True Tales of Terror
in the
Caves of the World

Also by Paul Jay Steward

Tales of Dirt, Danger, and Darkness

True Tales of Terror in the Caves of the World

Paul Jay Steward

CAVE BOOKS

Published by CAVE BOOKS
4700 Amberwood Drive
Dayton, Ohio 45424
www.cavebooks.com

CAVE BOOKS is the publications affiliate of the Cave Research Foundation.

Editors: Elizabeth Winkler, Paul Jay Steward
Publisher: Roger McClure
Layout: Paul Jay Steward
Cover Graphic Design: Gary Berdeaux
Cover Photograph: Kevin Downey

"Suicide Cave" by Ed Dejean was reprinted with permission from the National Speleological Society.

Library of Congress Cataloging-in-Publication Data

Steward, Paul Jay.
  True tales of terror in the caves of the world / Paul Jay Steward.
      p. cm.
  Includes bibliographical references.
  ISBN 0-939748-61-4 (pbk. : alk. paper)
  1. Crime--History--Case studies. 2. Murder--History--Case studies. 3. Caves. I. Title.

HV6251.S73 2004
364.1'0914'4--dc22

                                    2004005530

For my wife, Diana, and my children, Danielle and Bryan. Thank you for tolerating my obsession with caves and for accompanying me into the darkness. Forgive me for any nightmares you may have.

Have respect unto the covenant, for the dark places of the Earth are full of the habitations of cruelty.
—Psalm 74:20

Contents

Preface

One of the first questions I am usually asked about cave exploration is, "Have you ever found any bodies?" Fortunately, I have never found a body or the bones from one; however, I have been in a number of caves where someone has met an untimely death, and it does make the dark passages seem a bit creepy.

Nowhere else on Earth are there places as awe-inspiring in beauty and wonder, yet at the same time mysterious and foreboding as caves. Their darkness has a way of seeping into our very souls, bringing on fears of impending doom that chill us to the bone.

Since the dawn of humankind, caves have been used for places of shelter and religious ceremonies, as a refuge from enemies, and for the mining of minerals. There are those among us who use these secretive voids of the Earth for the evilest of deeds. Their hearts are as cold as the caves are dark. To these twisted individuals, the underground is the perfect place to hide the spoils of their work, far beyond the eyes of law and justice—a place where light and life seldom visit. Many believe that the underworld is also home to the Devil. Judging from the stories in this book, that idea may not be far from the truth.

As I wrote this page, on a whim I scanned the web and found the following story from Rio de Janeiro: "The cave served as the venue for killings in which the victims' bodies were squeezed into several car tires filled with gasoline and set on fire." It never ends. For as long as caves exist, someone will use them for places of unspeakable horror. And I, of course, will have another book to write.

MURDER AND MAYHEM

LOBELIA SALTPETER CAVE
West Virginia

On June 11, 1975, the body of Walter Smith was found in Lobelia Saltpeter Cave, Hillsboro, West Virginia. Smith was nineteen years old and had been missing for seven days. Acting on evidence found nearby, West Virginia State Police suspected the body might be found in the cave. The police realized they were neither equipped nor trained for cave exploration, so they asked local cavers to assist in the search.

At approximately 7:00 p.m., six cavers entered Lobelia Saltpeter Cave. Within minutes, they discovered Smith's nude body buried under a pile of rocks one hundred feet from the entrance. A blanket and plastic bag were wrapped around his head and secured with bailing twine, along with a rope tied around his chest. An autopsy revealed that Smith had been sexually assaulted and shot once in the neck and twice in the forehead with a .25 caliber weapon. With the discovery of the body, the state police and the FBI launched a murder investigation that reached deep into the caving community.

Their prime suspect was twenty-nine-year-old Peter

Hauer, a well-known and respected caver who owned the cave in which Smith was found. Hauer was a distinguished cave historian who had earned several National Speleological Society awards for his research of saltpeter caves. His gentle and quiet nature was a sharp contrast to the facts regarding the case and the charges brought against him. To this day, many remain skeptical of the handling of the investigation, the evidence, and the people involved. It is a bizarre tale that raises more questions than answers, and for those who will talk about it, no two tell the same account.

The story began in August 1970 when Peter Hauer purchased Lobelia Saltpeter Cave and moved from his home in Pennsylvania to West Virginia. The cave contains several levels totaling more than two thousand feet of passage. The history of the cave dates back to the Civil War when it was used as a source of saltpeter to make gunpowder.

Owning the cave was a dream come true for Hauer. As a retired schoolteacher, he planned to build a new house on his property and to earn a living off the land, but things quickly turned sour. A nearby landowner had also wanted the property that Hauer had bought, causing immediate tensions between them. Hauer also encountered hostilities from locals who did not take kindly to newcomers.

Within months of Hauer's moving into his new home, his fences were destroyed; his animals disappeared; his horse was lamed; his goats were savagely gutted and their throats slit, or their ears cut off and placed on fence posts. He feared for his own life and spent weeks away from his farm living with friends. For his safety, he bought a .25 caliber handgun and slept with the lights on. Tensions eventually eased, although Hauer never felt safe again.

On June 7, 1975, the parents of Walter Smith filed a missing persons report on their son, whom they could not locate. Smith worked as a lifeguard at Watoga State Park where he lived with a roommate. Three days earlier, Smith had written a letter to his roommate. In it he stated he was going for a bike ride and probably would return later.

In Smith's room, the police found a map of the Lobelia area and the names of several local residents. Smith had an interest in cults and had been interviewing members of local cults and communes to learn of their beliefs. Reporters following the case immediately picked up on this and suggested that Smith's disappearance might be associated with witchcraft or a satanic cult. The police extensively interviewed friends of Smith, along with several cult members and a close friend of his who claimed she was a witch.

The search was expanded to the Hillsboro area. Local hospitals were checked to determine whether Smith had been involved in an accident. Gradually, clues began to emerge. According to one witness, Smith was seen on June 5 riding his yellow ten-speed Schwinn bicycle in the Lobelia area. In a phone interview, Peter Hauer told a Watoga State Park Conservation Officer that Smith had visited his home on June 4, but left that evening. Hauer told friends that he was concerned about the missing boy and again talked of fear for his own life. During the investigation, the police stopped and questioned a man riding a bike that matched the description of Smith's. The police later identified the man as Hauer.

Twice on June 9, the police went to Hauer's residence to question him. During both visits he was not at home, but the rear door to his house was open and the lights were on inside. They returned to Hauer's property on

June 10 and again found nobody home, the rear door still open, and the lights still on.

On June 11, a search inside Hauer's house revealed a typed "Last Will and Testament" allegedly written and signed by Peter Hauer. In the document, Hauer confessed to killing Smith and stated that Smith's body was in the cave behind his house. He also stated that he was going to commit suicide and his body would be difficult to find. The letter contained numerous cross-outs and misspellings, contrary to the style of a schoolteacher. Forensics determined that the letter was typed on the typewriter found in Hauer's house and handwriting samples confirmed his signature. The police also found in his house a T-shirt and jeans stained with blood and dirt, and pieces of rope and plastic similar to those used in the crime. In an effort to find Hauer or any more evidence, hundreds of cavers, police, and National Guardsmen searched the surrounding hills, including more than one hundred caves. Divers searched two large ponds and drained another, but nothing was found.

Hauer's friends refused to believe he would kill someone or take his own life, and they were also skeptical of the letter that the police found. Many believed that Hauer was still alive, or that he also was a victim of foul play. Rumors surfaced that Hauer may have been kidnapped by a coven and was to be sacrificed during the coming equinox, or that he had fled to Brazil. Until a body was found, the police also believed he might still be alive.

The FBI sent agents to look for Hauer at the National Speleological Society's annual convention held that year in June at Angels Camp, California, but he did not appear. The summer months passed with the mystery of Peter Hauer still haunting the police and Hauer's friends. Confident that more clues would emerge, the state police and the FBI continued the search. They questioned more than one hundred people, but learned little more.

On November 27, 1975, a father and son were deer hunting in the hills, approximately one mile from Hauer's property, when they spotted the remains of a human body, hanging from the end of a rope, high in a tree. A pile of bones lay on the ground. Forensic experts collected the bones and sent them to the Chief Medical Examiner, who confirmed what was already suspected. Based on dental records and X-rays, he was certain that the remains were those of Peter Hauer and that the cause of death was suicide. The police closed the case, ruling that Peter Hauer murdered Walter Smith and then committed suicide. The motive for the crime was said to be mental illness.

On December 13, 1975, close friends of Hauer's gathered at his home for a memorial service. Atop a hill on the property, each person placed a stone on the grave that contained Hauer's ashes. Later that day, a formal funeral service was held in the nearby town.

The police logged more than 6,000 miles and 825 hours on the investigation, yet they found little evidence. Hauer's house and property were thoroughly searched several times; however, the police never found the amount of blood one would expect from a crime of this nature. In the days following the discovery of the body, hundreds of people tramped over the crime scene, reducing the chances of finding any small clues. Neither the gun used in the crime nor Hauer's gun was ever recovered, and the clothes, glasses, and bicycle belonging to Walter Smith were never found. Even the police reports are confusing and contain numerous omissions. Friends speak of Hauer as a gentle man, incapable of murder. Many want to believe that Hauer's signature on the Last

Will and Testament was forged and that he was taken away against his will. If this is true, the thought of an unsolved double murder is just as unsettling.

In February 1977, Marshall Fausold bought the cave from the Hauer family. In 1979, the National Speleological Society established the Peter M. Hauer Spelean History Award. This award was instituted to recognize significant accomplishments in spelean history. In 1998, Fausold donated the cave and surrounding 29.5 acres of land to the Southeastern Cave Conservancy. On the property is a granite memorial giving tribute to Hauer and his love for caves and caving.

BLACKMAN CAVE
Japan

On Saturday, July 1, 2000, Lucie Blackman met a man for a lunch date and a drive to the Chiba coast on Tokyo Bay. At 7:00 p.m., she phoned her roommate, Linda Phillips, to say she would be home in half an hour. It was the last time anyone heard from Lucie. After a worry-filled weekend, Phillips called the police.

Lucie Blackman had come to Tokyo from England two months prior to her disappearance. Her plans were to stay for a few months to earn enough money for a trip to Australia. She was a strikingly beautiful former British Airways stewardess with blond hair, blue eyes, and sophisticated manners. Upon her arrival to Japan, she found work in a hostess bar where girls were paid to chat, flirt, and drink with Japanese businessmen. Popular girls could earn up to $400 a night in these posh nightclubs. Many of the clubs required the girls to go on dohans (dates) outside business hours for lunches and dinners.

On that day in July, Lucie went on a dohan and was never seen again.

The search for Lucie was one of the largest police investigations in Tokyo's history. Her picture and news of her disappearance were broadcast across Japan in an effort to find her, but few clues were found.

After three frustrating months, a break finally came. In a case unrelated to Blackman's, the police arrested 48-year-old Joji Obara, a Japanese real estate millionaire. Obara was charged with sexual assault and rape. It was alleged that he had a nasty habit of drugging women into unconsciousness and then videotaping himself raping them. More than one hundred tapes were collected from his house. When questioned about Lucie, he denied any involvement with her. But further investigation revealed that she had made a call from one of his cell phones, and strands of her blond hair were found in his apartment. Other phone records showed that two days after Lucie disappeared there was a seven-hour gap during which Obara made no calls. A picture of her, showing the sea in the background, was found on a roll of film from his camera. The camera automatically dated the picture on July 1. Obara owned an apartment near the beach, prompting the police to again search the coastal areas.

During the investigation, the police had looked into a small, narrow sea cave fifteen feet from the water's edge and a few hundred feet from Obara's apartment. The cave contained garbage and an overturned tub that no one had bothered to investigate.

On February 9, eight months after the report of Lucie's disappearance, the police returned to the cave. Buried beneath the tub, they found several bags that contained the badly decayed and dismembered body of Lucie Blackman. Her nude body was cut into eight pieces, and her head was encased in a cement block. Following the gruesome discovery, friends and locals paid their respects to Lucie by adorning the cave entrance with flowers, cards, fruits, and burning incense.

As the police began to piece the bizarre crime together, it was noted that Obara had purchased a chainsaw and cement mix on July 3 from a local hardware store. Also that afternoon, the police were summoned to Obara's apartment after receiving a call that a tenant was acting suspiciously. Obara greeted the officers with cement mix on his hands. He said he was working in the bathroom—the one room he would not allow them to look into. That night, Obara was seen pacing along the beach near the cave. The next day, Obara was treated at a hospital for extensive bug bites he had received the previous night. Even after all this, months passed before Obara was considered a suspect in the case.

The police believe that Lucie died from an overdose of drugs administered by Obara who then hastily disposed of the body. In April 2001, Obara was charged with raping and causing the death of Lucie Blackman. As of March 2004, the outcome of the case was undetermined.

CARLSBAD CAVERNS
New Mexico

In 1901, Jim White explored a cave in southeastern New Mexico known to local farmers as the Bat Cave. Using a kerosene lamp, White explored farther and farther into the depths of the huge cavern. His friends thought he was crazy, and he found it difficult to convince others to follow him into the cave. Not until the 1920s did the stories of his discoveries finally reach the public through newspapers across the country. Today, the cave is known as Carlsbad Caverns. Millions of people have since visited the cave, making it one of the nation's top tourist attractions. On July 10, 1979, four men entered the cave to add a new chapter to its already long history.

At approximately 3:00 p.m., Dennis Mark, Eugene Meroney, William Lovejoy, and David Kuczynski purchased tickets for a cavern tour at the Carlsbad Caverns National Park Visitor Center. Both Meroney and Lovejoy walked somewhat stiff-legged, and each used one crutch as they proceeded toward the east elevator lobby.

After a short wait, the quartet boarded the elevator along with Park Technician Linda Phillips. Linda was a librarian from Tennessee and was working at the park for the summer. Celia Valdez, a ten-year Park Service employee who was operating the elevator, checked the tickets of the four men, closed the door, and started the 750-foot descent to the cavern floor.

During the ride, Celia overheard one of the men whisper, "We'll do it now." As she turned toward the voice, the men pulled out several guns that were concealed under their clothing. Within seconds, both Celia and Linda were looking down the barrels of a twelve-gauge shotgun, two Winchester rifles, and a Ruger pistol. The men also carried eight hundred rounds of ammunition. In the men's rush to uncover their weapons, shotgun shells and a bottle of whiskey fell to the floor.

The women were ordered not to touch any of the controls and to continue the descent. The men said they were taking over the cave and that both Celia and Linda were now their hostages. Upon reaching the bottom, Linda was forced out of the elevator and taken to the

Information Booth in the underground Lunchroom. She was ordered to announce over the PA system that the approximately two hundred tourists in the area were to leave the cave on foot as quickly as possible up the Main Corridor to the cave's natural entrance.

Celia was held in the elevator and told to phone the surface to explain that the cave was being taken over. After the call, Celia was pushed out of the elevator with a gun to her back. Walking slightly ahead of her captors, she escaped by disappearing into the rush of people running to exit the cave.

At 3:10 p.m., Area Park Manager Jack Linahan called down to the Lunchroom, but the gunmen refused to talk on the phone. They wanted to meet with Linahan in person to hear their demands, stating they were "prepared to die." As Linahan got off the elevator, Dennis Mark and another man met him with guns drawn. Mark, the ringleader, did most of the talking. He demanded that a newspaper reporter be sent down to them. They also wanted one million dollars and an airplane to fly them safely to Brazil. Linda Phillips would be released unharmed after their demands were met. They also said they had dynamite and threatened to blow up portions of the cave. After negotiating with the gunmen, Linahan was allowed to return to the surface along with the remaining tourists from the Lunchroom. Unknown to the whiskey-swilling cavenappers, ninety-nine tourists and six Park Service employees decided to remain hidden two thousand feet away at the Top of the Cross located in the Big Room.

On the surface, Linahan continued to negotiate with the outlaws. He called Ned Cantwell, the publisher of the Carlsbad Current-Argus newspaper, to come to help. Outside the cave, state and local police, sheriff's officers,

FBI personnel, and news reporters began to arrive. Guards were posted throughout the park, and all the roads were closed to unauthorized personnel.

At 4:40 p.m., Ned Cantwell arrived at the cave. The gunmen refused to talk on the phone to Cantwell and told him to "get your ass down here." They promised him he would not be hurt, but Cantwell stalled for time. The gunmen were drunk and restless and passed the time by shooting their guns. They felt certain they were going to be killed and wanted to get their story out to the world before the police and FBI stormed the cave. At 5:20 p.m., Cantwell finally agreed to meet the gunmen and nervously rode down the elevator to the Lunchroom.

When the elevator door opened, Cantwell was met by Kuczynski and Meroney. At gunpoint, Cantwell was pushed against the wall and searched for weapons, but he was carrying only a pad, pencil, and a tape recorder. They escorted him to the Information Booth, where Dennis Mark was waiting.

This was what the men were waiting for—and the real reason they had taken over the cave—someone to hear their complaints and relay them to the world. They were frustrated and wanted to "wake the American people up." They complained about inflation, gas shortages, politics, government, and the recession. Lovejoy and Meroney were Native Americans and wanted recognition for the Indian people. They were tired of having Mexicans take their jobs. Their words were slurred, and they rambled on without a concise message. The men had known each other only for a few days, and it was apparent that the cavenapping was ill-planned. At one point, the gunmen asked for a bottle of whiskey in exchange for Linda and Cantwell but were refused. They continued to phone the surface to talk to Linahan about their demands for money and an airplane. They even called their friends to boast about the takeover.

After several hours of negotiations, the gunmen offered to allow Linda and Cantwell to return to the surface in exchange for misdemeanor charges. Although the FBI refused to make promises, Linda and Cantwell were released unharmed.

Unknown to the gunmen, the group of tourists hiding in the back of the cave were listening on another phone to the conversations between the gunmen and the surface. They were also talking to the surface. The ordeal of being trapped in a cold, dark cave was beginning to take its toll. Among the group was a Park Service employee on her first day on the job, and she had forgotten to bring her medication. She was having epileptic convulsions and might not survive without medical help. There was also concern for two diabetics who had not brought their insulin. In the group was a deaf couple with a hungry infant. A nursing mother, whose baby was left on the surface, tried to breast-feed the child but was unsuccessful. Not until the ordeal was over did the deaf couple fully understand the situation.

At 8:00 p.m., Dennis Mark agreed to return to the surface to negotiate face-to-face with Special Agent Ron Hoatson. Because of growing concerns about the trapped tourists, Mark was told that if the remaining gunmen surrendered, they would be charged only with federal misdemeanor charges. Mark agreed to this and called down for his three friends to come up.

At 8:47 p.m., FBI agents took all four gunmen away. Within minutes of the gunmen's surrender, medical personnel, park rangers, and FBI agents entered the cave to help the trapped party return to the surface and to secure the crime scene.

Agents found that more than two hundred rounds of gunshots had damaged much of the Lunchroom area. The reputed six cases of dynamite were never located. At 11:00 p.m., reporters were allowed to view the crime scene.

Although the siege lasted less than six hours, it took weeks for state and federal prosecutors, arguing over jurisdiction, to decide what charges to bring against the men. The state called the men terrorists and pressed for charges of kidnapping and aggravated assault. They feared that a misdemeanor charge would only encourage other criminals. The government was hesitant to renege on the promise of misdemeanor charges, fearing this would hinder future negotiations in similar situations. In the end, federal prosecutors prevailed and issued misdemeanor charges.

On August 2, 1979, Dennis Mark, Eugene Meroney, William Lovejoy, and David Kuczynski pleaded guilty to damaging government property and to aiding and abetting in the damage of government property. The charge carried a $1,000 fine and a maximum of one year in jail.

For their role in resolving the cavern takeover, Linda Phillips, Jack Linaham, and Ned Cantwell received certificates of appreciation from the city and the National Park Service. President Jimmy Carter personally commended Ned Cantwell for his acts of heroism.

SAWNEY BEANE CAVE
Scotland

S awney Beane was born in 1547 near Edinburgh, Scotland. His parents worked hard and raised their only son the best they could. But even at an early age, Sawney was a troubled child with few friends. As he grew older, he developed a vicious temper and resented authority of any kind. Crime came easy for Sawney, and earning an honest living was never a choice he would make in life.

Sawney wanted no part of the life his parents thought best for him. He married a young girl with an equally vicious personality, and they moved to the Scottish seacoast of Galloway. There they found residence in a large sea cave. The cave was more than one mile long with many side passages. Twice a day, the tide flooded two hundred yards into the cave and completely obscured the low entrance. The cave also provided a safe haven from which to operate their nightly raids of robbery and murder.

They preyed upon unwary travelers along the dark roads between villages, and it was their policy to murder everyone they robbed. They stripped their victims of clothing, jewelry, and other valuables, and tossed the bodies into the sea.

News about the missing people spread across the country. Out of fear, people moved away, and the region became deserted. Local villagers panicked and, in haste, executed several innocent people thought responsible for these crimes. Still, people continued to disappear. King James VI of Scotland was so concerned that he sent spies to the area, only to have them vanish without a trace.

Sawney and his wife eventually had children, but they found it increasing difficult to provide enough food for this growing family. One day the Beanes had a grand idea. They would use the flesh from the people they had killed to feed their children. From that day forward, all their victims were brought to the cave.

The bodies were cut into pieces to be dried, salted, and pickled. Food was plentiful once again. This lifestyle lasted the Beanes twenty-five years while they raised eight sons and six daughters who, by incest, produced a total of thirty-two grandchildren. The whole family lived in the cave, and all were raised on crime and human consumption.

Hunting like packs of wild dogs, the Beanes grew more brazen in the frequency of their killings. Before, they had killed for survival, but now it was merely for the thrill, and although they were all well trained, it was only a matter of time until they made a grave mistake.

According to the legend, one night a man and wife on horseback were returning from a nearby fair. The Beanes surrounded the pair and seized the woman. Within seconds, she was stripped and disemboweled. Like beasts, they drank her blood. The man fought desperately for his life, and just as he, too, was about to be pulled from his horse, another group of twenty or more, returning from the fair, came upon the scene. Knowing they were outnumbered, the Beanes retreated in haste through the woods to the safety of their cave.

The man and his wife's remains were taken to the Magistrate of Glasgow. The following day, more than four hundred soldiers, with twenty-four dogs, gathered in what was the largest manhunt in Scottish history. Led by King James himself, they spread out across the Galloway countryside in search of the horrid group.

They searched for days with no luck. Several times they passed by the cave, yet thought nothing of this water-filled hole. Finally, during low tide, the dogs ran into the cave barking and howling wildly. The men followed with torches lit and swords drawn, checking every place that one could hide. After several thousand feet they came to a large room.

Hanging from the walls and ceiling were the arms,

legs, hands, feet, and bodies of men, women, and children. Other rooms contained huge barrels of body parts being pickled in brine. Realizing they had to act quickly or find themselves trapped by high tide, they let the dogs loose into the darkness. In a matter of minutes, the dogs had Sawney and his family cornered in the back of the cave. The entire family of forty-eight men, women, and children were seized and marched back to Edinburg. The remains of the dead were buried outside the cave.

Although King James VI was instrumental in establishing a court system, he felt this horde did not merit due process of law. Every one of the Beanes was raised to regard murder, incest, and cannibalism as normal ways of life. Isolated from society, they saw no wrong in what they did. The entire clan was sentenced to a painful execution without the benefit of a trial.

To suit their crimes, the males were dismembered; their hands and legs were severed, and they were left to slowly bleed to death while the women were forced to watch. Afterwards, three fires were made into which the women were thrown alive. At no time during the executions did the Beanes express any signs of repentance or remorse for the people they had killed. It is suspected that Sawney and his family murdered more than one thousand people. They also have the distinction of being listed in an early edition of the *Guinness Book of World Records* as one of the largest bands of murderous cannibals who ever walked the Earth. An anonymous author wrote the following song about the Beanes.

The Ballad of Sawney Beane

Go ye not by Galloway
Come bide awhile, my friend

I'll tell ye of the dangers there
Beware of Sawney Beane.
There's nobody knows that he bides there
For his face is seldom seen
But to meet his eye is to meet your fate
At the hands of Sawney Beane.
For Sawney he has taken a wife
And he's hungry babes to wean
And he's raised them up on the flesh of men
In the cave of Sawney Beane.
And Sawney has been well endowed
With daughters young and lean
And they have taken their father's seed
In the cave of Sawney Beane.
And Sawney's sons are young and strong
And their blades are sharp and keen
To spill the blood of travelers
What meet with Sawney Beane.
So if you ride from there to here
Be ye wary in between
Lest they catch your horse and spill your blood
In the cave of Sawney Beane.
They'll hang ye up and cut your throat
An they'll pick your carcass clean
An they'll give your bones to the little ones
In the cave of Sawney Beane.
But fear ye not, our Captain rides
On an errand of the Queen
And he carries the writ of fire and sword
For the head of Sawney Beane.
They've hung them high in Edinburgh town
And likewise all their kin
And the wind blows cold on their bones
For to Hell they all have gone.

HARITON CAVE
Israel

On the morning of May 9, 2001, Kobi Mandell and Yossi Ishran skipped school to spend the day hiking in the Judean Desert. In 1996, Kobi and his family had immigrated to Israel from College Park, Maryland. Later, they moved to the Jewish West Bank settlement of Tekoa, where the two boys met and became good friends.

After buying provisions, the boys set off into an area of the desert known as the Wadi Hariton. The Wadi is a popular area for tourists and is known for an abundance of caves, ancient ruins, and dried-up riverbeds. It was the perfect place for two teenagers eager to explore. One of the attractions is Hariton Cave, the longest in Israel, with more than two miles of passage. Occupation of the cave dates back to the nineteenth century when it was used for shelter by Christian hermits.

When the boys did not return home by nightfall, their worried parents notified the police. Teams of police, soldiers, and local residents, using torches and night-vision goggles, searched the desert throughout the night. By morning, the boys' bodies were found bound together under a pile of stones in the entrance of Hariton Cave. They had been bludgeoned to death with bowling ball-sized rocks. Their blood was smeared on the cave walls and used to write slogans. The bodies were so badly mutilated that family members could not identify them. Forensic experts suspect the boys were tortured for more than two hours before they finally died. Three assailants are believed to have been responsible for the attack.

After the bodies were removed, several ultra-orthodox Jews scraped the blood off the walls. Jewish custom requires that all bodily remains, including blood, be buried.

The police believe that the killings may be linked to the theft of ninety goats from the community the previous night. Others think that the crime is related to the Israeli-Palestinian conflict that has plagued the area for years. Settlements such as Tekoa are illegal under an international law that forbids conquering powers from settling captured land. Regardless of ownership, for the 225 families living in Tekoa, Hariton Cave will always be a haunting reminder of human brutality.

ESCAPE CAVE
Alcatraz Island

Two and a half miles off the California coast, Alcatraz Island rises out of the cold and murky waters of the San Francisco Bay. The island, also known as "The Rock," is home to America's most celebrated prison: Alcatraz Federal Penitentiary. Here the worst of the worst were sent to pay their debt to society. For twenty-nine years, it held 1,545 prisoners. Notorious criminals such as Al Capone, Machine-Gun Kelly, Doc Barker, Alvin Karpis, and Robert Stroud (the Bird-Man of Alcatraz) all did their time on The Rock.

Atop the island's plateau sits a massive white cellblock that stands out in sharp contrast to the sheer, dark sandstone cliffs that meet the ocean. These cliffs, along with barbed wire, armed guards, rip tides, and a long, cold swim, are formidable barriers that hinder most plans for escape.

From the time it became a federal prison in 1933 to its close in 1963, fourteen escape attempts involving thirty-six men have taken place. Officially, no one has ever successfully escaped from Alcatraz, although five prisoners are listed as missing and presumed dead. Of the remaining thirty-one, twenty-three were caught, six were shot and killed, and two drowned. One of the men who almost escaped, with the help of a cave, was Floyd Hamilton.

As one of Bonnie and Clyde's henchmen, Hamilton terrorized the American southwest with numerous hold-ups and bank robberies and held the FBI's prime spot of Public Enemy Number One before being captured in 1938. He was considered extremely dangerous and had previously escaped from a Texas jail. Now, at age thirty-six, he was not about to sit peacefully on The Rock for the next thirty years.

On April 14, 1943, Hamilton, along with fellow convicts James Boarman, Harold Brest, and Fred Hunter, made a desperate, early morning fight for freedom. Armed with prison-made knives, they overpowered, tied up, and gagged the Custodial Officer and Captain of the Guards, Henry Weinhold. Then, barefoot and wearing only underwear, the men leapt from a window to the rocky shore thirty feet below. Landing unharmed, they dove into the chilly bay water.

Within seconds of their escape, Captain Weinhold wriggled free of his bonds. Another officer saw the gang fleeing and sounded the alarm. The quartet was twenty yards off shore when the first bullets rained down from the guards posted in the high towers. Hamilton and Hunter instantly went under, while Boarman and Brest continued swimming out into the foggy bay. A patrol boat was launched and quickly came alongside the two swimmers. As Brest was pulled into the boat, Boarman's mortally wounded body disappeared beneath the waves.

The police and Coast Guard immediately surrounded the island and began searching for what they thought would be three bodies washed ashore. Within hours, bloodstains were found on the rocks near one of the many small sea caves that dotted the island's shoreline. Inside the cave, Hunter was found cowering amid trash and debris.

The two missing prisoners were not found by nightfall. Warden James A. Johnson said, "We will probably never find the bodies of the other two. Sometimes bodies come up in the bay after nine days, sometimes after thirty days—but usually they don't come up at all." Speaking of Floyd Hamilton's death, Johnson replied, "We're positive that Hamilton is dead. He was shot, and we saw him go under."

Unknown to prison officials, Hamilton was not dead. He had found his way back to shore unscathed and was hiding in the same cave Hunter had used. That night, he tried to swim across the bay but, discouraged by cold water and strong currents, returned to the cave. There he hid in a small side passage to gather his strength for another attempt.

Hamilton was miserable in the cave. High tide flooded his cramped quarters, sharp rocks scraped his skin, and bugs and crabs bit at his flesh. The following night, he again tried to swim across the bay but found it impossible to succeed. After hiding in the cave for two days and suffering from cold, fatigue, and hunger, he was a broken man. Hamilton managed to climb the steep cliff face and reenter the prison through the same bar-spread window from which the four desperados had escaped.

In the morning, Hamilton willingly surrendered after being found half-hidden under a pile of clothing in a prison storeroom. His face and body had cuts and bruises, and his hair was caked with dirt and dried salt. Ironically, it was Captain Weinhold who found him.

Floyd Hamilton never attempted another escape. He became a model prisoner and was released in 1958 after serving fifteen more years. He went on to write a book about his life of crime called *Public Enemy No. 1* and has a book-on-tape about his life with Bonnie and Clyde called *Bonnie and Clyde and Me*.

Because of needed restoration and increasing maintenance costs, Alcatraz Prison was closed on March 21, 1963. The island was opened to the public in 1973 as a part of the Golden Gate National Recreation Area. Today, it is one of the most visited of National Park Service sites. Here tourists get a glimpse of an era when robbing banks and toting Thomson submachine guns made heroes out of a few bad guys.

FOSTER CAVE
South Africa

The history of crime in South Africa is filled with colorful and notorious figures. Although few criminals gained the notoriety of their counterparts in North America, they were just as violent. One of the most lawless was William Foster, leader of the infamous Foster Gang. For more than a year, Foster and his men wreaked havoc with a series of violent robberies and murders. During their campaign of terror, this mob rose to the unsavory distinction of Public Enemy Number One and instigated one of the largest manhunts ever conducted by South African police.

William Foster was born in 1886 and grew up in East Griqualand, South Africa. As an adult, he was a devoted father and husband. Beneath his pleasant demeanor, however, was a hot-tempered man, resentful of most authority. His first brushes with the law were minor, but with each occurrence the severity of the crime increased. In 1913, Foster met John Maxim, and together with Jack Johnson, and Foster's brother, Jimmy, they planned their first armed robbery of the American Swiss Watch Company.

Disguised with fake beards and moustaches, the foursome entered the store at the close of business and bound and gagged the two shop owners. They ransacked the store and escaped with thousands of dollars worth of rings, watches, and jewelry. Within months, all but Maxim were caught and sent to jail.

Nine months later, Foster escaped from prison. He teamed up with his old pal, John Maxim, and the duo added Cari Mezar to their gang. This trio immediately began a crime spree the likes of which South African police had never seen. During the next three months, they robbed two post offices, a bank, and a liquor store, leaving a wake of death in their path. Twice the men narrowly escaped capture in a blaze of guns and bloodshed with Foster being wounded and three police officers killed.

On September 17, 1914, the hunt for the Foster Gang intensified. Roadblocks were set up across Johannesburg, and every available policeman became involved in the search. The gang's getaway car was found abandoned on a dirt road. Bloodhounds hot on a scent led the police to a small cave in the Kensington hills. The cave was immediately surrounded, and large rocks were rolled across the entrance. Hundreds of sightseers eager to see a shootout swarmed the area. As a young child, Foster had played in this very cave. Now its walls had become his prison.

From above the entrance, the police attempted to

lower canisters of tear gas into the cave, but the wind blew the smoke into the crowd. The police anticipated that the men might make a break from the cave. Floodlights illuminated the entrance at night as police and onlookers watched and waited.

The following morning, as the police removed some of the rocks, a single gunshot was heard coming from inside the cave. Cari Mezar had committed suicide. Shortly after Mezar's death, Foster appeared at the entrance and said he would surrender only after he had talked to his wife. To avoid any more bloodshed, the police agreed to his wishes.

Peggy Foster arrived at the scene with their five-month-old daughter, and together they entered the cave. Half an hour later, William Foster appeared at the entrance again and requested to talk to his mother and father and two sisters, who were also present. Foster wanted to say goodbye to them. He and Maxim had formed a suicide pact to avoid a hanging. Peggy decided she could not live without her husband and joined in the pact. She handed their child to Foster's sister, and the fugitives returned to the cave. Several minutes later, three shots rang out from the cave. As the chosen executioner, Maxim shot Foster and his wife and then turned the gun on himself to end the standoff and the Foster Gang's reign of crime.

MASSACRE CAVE
Isle of Eigg

The Isle of Eigg lies ten miles off the western coast of Scotland. Approximately five miles long and three miles wide, it is easily distinguishable by the sheer one thousand-foot cliffs that surround most of its plateau. Its craggy shoreline is dotted with numerous caves. One of the largest is Cathedral Cave, a place in which the Jacobite Catholics secretly congregated to celebrate mass. Another cave infamous in the island's history is Massacre Cave. This cave, located along the southern shore, became so named after the island's entire population was brutally murdered in it.

Occupation of the island dates to 2000 BC, and it boasts a rich and sometimes turbulent past. Its shores have been home to Vikings and Norse settlers, who used the island as an important base for trading. In medieval times, it was owned by Ranald MacDonald, a descendant of Somerled, the Norse/Irish King of the Isles. Years of Scottish warfare on the island developed into a bitter feud between the MacDonald and the MacLeod clans. One of the most tragic confrontation between these two occurred in 1577.

While sailing along the coast of Scotland, a small party of MacLeods were blown off course and took shelter on the Isle of Eigg. The island's population was predominantly MacDonald. When no one offered the stranded men food or shelter, they became angry and raped some of the women. The unruly men were immediately captured. Several MacLeods were killed during the fight, leaving three survivors who were tied up, castrated, and set adrift in their own boat. Days later, the men were found barely alive drifting along the shore of Scotland.

The MacLeod Chief was enraged after he heard what happened to his men. To avenge this deed, he gathered his best fighters and sailed to Eigg. The islanders saw the huge force coming and sought refuge in a deep cave with a narrow entrance hidden behind a small waterfall. For three days, the people of Eigg hid in the cave. Frustrated and confused at not finding a single person, the MacLeods returned to their ships. In haste, a MacDonald left the cave and climbed atop a high crest to watch the departing ships. He was seen, and the boats immediately turned around.

During their stay in the cave, a light snow had fallen on the island. The invading MacLeods marched up the hill and simply followed the footprints of the lone lookout to the cave. They demanded that those responsible for setting their men adrift come forward. When no one came forth, the MacLeods decided to smoke them out. From above, a group of men diverted the waterfall. Others piled brushwood, heather, and timbers in front of the entrance, and set it ablaze. The wet grasses burned with a thick smoke that was directed into the cave, but not a single MacDonald surrendered or tried to escape. They knew their fate in the hands of the MacLeods would be far worse than their dying a suffocating death in a smoke-filled cave. By nightfall, the fire was extinguished and several men entered the cave. What they found shocked even the murderers. In the gloom, their torchlights revealed the remains of the island's entire population of 398 men, women, and children.

The bones remained unburied for centuries. In 1845, one visitor said the cave resembled a charnel house and wrote: "At almost every step we came upon human bones." Skulls were prized souvenirs of trips to the island until someone decided that the remains should have a proper burial. As recently as twenty years ago, a child's skull was found in the cave. In 1993, bones found in storage at the Campbeltown Museum were believed to be from the cave and were returned to a descendant of the clan.

Approximately sixty people live on the island today. Tourism is a big part of the island's economy, and a trip to Eigg would not be complete without a hike to the island's premier attraction, Massacre Cave.

DUNGEON CAVE
Czech Republic

During the thirteenth century, an unsavory thief built a castle along a popular travel route near the town of Blansko, Czechoslovakia. The castle was constructed over the entrance shaft of a large cave, which made a convenient place to dispose of anyone who opposed the owner's means of business. A forty-foot drop into the cave usually killed the victims. Those who survived the fall faced a slow death by starvation.

In the 1850s, explorers found thousands of bones covering the cave floor. The bones were collected to make soap and other industrial materials. Today, the cave is called Hladomorna Jeskyne or Dungeon Cave. The English translation of Hladomorna is "kill by hunger."

The castle ruins are a popular stop for tourists. Cavers recently discovered another entrance to the cave that could have served as an escape route. Many believe that the area is haunted and that the moans of the victims can still be heard.

CAVE OF THE PATRIARCHS
Hebron

The Cave of the Patriarchs, also known as Machpelah Cave, or the Tomb of the Patriarchs, has been the site of considerable violence and bloodshed. It is located south of Jerusalem in the town of Hebron. Today, Hebron is largely an Arab community, but it is also the location of the oldest Jewish settlement in the world.

The cave is mentioned eight times in the Bible Book of Genesis, and it is the oldest and one of the holiest sites in the Jewish religion. It is said that the Patriarchs Abraham, Isaac, and Jacob, along with the Matriarchs Sarah, Rebecca, and Leah, are buried in the cave. The cave is also believed to contain a passageway to the Garden of Eden.

Above the cave stands a huge temple built almost two thousand years ago by Herod, King of Judea. Claims about who actually owns the land have caused continuous conflicts. For now, the cave remains under Muslim jurisdiction, but the Israeli Army guards the site.

Both Jews and Muslims trace their ancestry back to Abraham, who bought the cave for a family tomb. Although restrictions are imposed on Jewish prayers, this location is one of the few places on Earth where Jews and Muslims worship in the same place. This, of course, causes hostilities to erupt frequently in the area. Over the years, hundreds of worshipers at the cave have been wounded or killed.

One of the bloodiest attacks at the cave occurred on the morning of February 25, 1994. Baruch Goldstein, a Jewish settler and immigrant from New York, opened fire on the backs of Muslim worshipers as they knelt in prayer in the temple. He continued shooting into the crowd of more than two hundred people until he was finally beaten to death. By then, he had killed twenty-nine and wounded one hundred and twenty-five. Many eyewitnesses say Goldstein, an Israeli soldier, did not act alone, although this was never proven.

The massacre spurred massive riots along the West Bank and Gaza Strip that killed twenty-five more people. Hebron is a city that has long been divided between areas of Israeli and Palestinian control, and at its core is the Cave of the Patriarchs.

CASTLE ROYAL CAVES
Minnesota

C aves and crime often go hand and hand. They have been used for murders, massacres, body dumpings, hideouts, and places to conceal stills and drug labs. The Castle Royal Caves, also known as the Wabasha Street Caves in Saint Paul, Minnesota, are among those most strongly associated with crime.

These caves consist of a series of seven large chambers that extend one hundred and fifty feet underground. In the mid-1800s, Minnesota immigrants excavated here for sandstone used for making roads throughout Saint Paul. Entrepreneurs found many uses for the empty caves. The cool and constant temperature underground was ideal for food storage, and for several years the caves housed a successful mushroom growing business. In 1933, they were converted into a ritzy nightclub complete with crystal chandeliers, oriental carpets, and expensive fixtures. Evening shows featured popular performers such as Cab Calloway and the Dorsey Brothers.

During the 1930s gangster era, Saint Paul was deemed a safe haven for criminals as long as they registered with authorities, paid a fee, and did not commit any crimes within the city limits. The system worked well for controlling crime and had the approval of local police and the FBI. Famed criminals such as Ma Barker, Baby

Face Nelson, John Dillinger, and assorted mob figures all frequented the Castle Royal nightclub. It was the perfect underworld for the underworld, but it did not take long for illegal gambling, bootleg liquor, prostitution, and murder to find its way inside.

One evening a cleaning lady witnessed the shooting of three gangsters in a back room of the nightclub and immediately called for help. When the police arrived, the woman was amazed to find the bodies and blood gone. The only clue the police found was a bullet-riddled stone wall. The bodies were never located and were believed to have been buried somewhere in the caves.

Shortly after the murders, rumors of ghosts in the caves began to circulate and have persisted to the present day. Employees and patrons have reported whispers, voices, strange noises, party sounds, big-band music, and sightings of spirits dressed in gangster era clothing. A ghost known as Georgie makes frequent appearances in the men's restroom, and a female ghost is sometimes seen drinking at the bar.

The caves and nightclub are still popular attractions among ghost hunters and historians. Banquet facilities are available, as well as tours of the caves. For anyone interested in caves, ghosts, gangsters, and a good meal, this is your nirvana.

CATAWBA MURDER HOLE
Virginia

During the late 1800s and early 1900s, traveling salesmen were common throughout the United States. Traveling by horse and buggy, they made their way from town to town, selling and trading their wares.

It was a lonely job as they were away from their friends and families for weeks at a time. It was also a dangerous job. They were forced to cross rough terrain and to travel in all kinds of weather. Many salesmen disappeared or were found along the roadside robbed and murdered.

On one occasion, a young salesman was on his way home to his wife and children after a prosperous journey. He had finished selling the last of his items to a farmer who lived on the outskirts of Catawba, Virginia. To help pay for the goods, the farmer offered the salesman a bed for the night and a breakfast the following morning. The salesman gladly accepted.

The morning dawned with dark skies and torrential rain. After breakfast, the farmer helped the man harness his horse and maneuver his buggy down the washed-out driveway. As they neared the main road, the farmer thought about all the money the young man must surely have. He hit the salesman on the head, knocking him unconscious, and stole all his money and valuables. Then he drove the horse, buggy, and salesman to the edge of a large sinkhole on his property.

This sinkhole was more than one hundred feet across and considered bottomless by locals. With one crack of his whip, the farmer sent the horse, the carriage, and the salesman plunging headlong into the dark abyss. News of the missing salesman spread across the state. His wife searched for months but never found her husband's body. Today, many believe that Catawba Murder Hole is where this horrible crime occurred.

Another story associated with Catawba Murder Hole is the tale of two young lovers whose families fought a bitter feud and refused to allow the two children to be together. Heartbroken over their separation, they could not bear to live apart. Late one night, they met at the cave's gaping entrance. There they chose to be united in death and jumped into the open blackness. Part of a song entitled "Legends of Murder Hole" by Marian McConnell tells about the cave.

One legend says that a tinker by trade
Was killed by a farmer for things that he made
The tinkerman's body and wagon and mule
Were hidden below by that greedy ol' fool
And old timers tell tales about a young girl
Who like Juliet, said farewell to the world
She threw herself off of that hundred-foot ledge
Her lover then followed her over the edge

Cavers have mapped more than one thousand feet of passage in Catawba Murder Hole and have plumbed the depths to more than two hundred and thirty feet. The remains of the salesman and the two lovers have not been found.

OUVEA CAVE
New Caledonia

Nine hundred miles off the northeast coast of Australia is a group of islands known as Kanaky, or New Caledonia, as British Captain Cook named them in 1775. The islands have been populated for more than three thousand years since the arrival of Melanesian Kanaks from Papua New Guinea. More than one hundred caves have been discovered here, many of them still unexplored.

New Caledonia is officially an overseas territory of France. Native Kanaks have a long history of resistance to French rule, starting as far back as 1843 when the islands were controlled by French Catholics. Over the years, numerous revolts and violent uprisings have taken place there in the fight for independence from France. One of the bloodiest confrontations occurred in a cave on the island of Ouvea.

On April 22, 1988, forty Kanaky youths attempted to raise the Kanak flag at a police headquarters. A fight broke out that resulted in the death of four French military police officers. The boys fled to the village of Gossannah, which was known for its strong support of independence for the Kanaky people, with twenty-seven officers as their hostages.

The elders of the tribe hid the boys and the hostages in one of the island's many caves. For two days, members of the tribe attempted in vain to stall the advance of French military troops. Captured villagers were locked up without food while negotiations took place for release of the hostages.

On the morning of May 4, 1988, French troops discovered the cave. With negotiations still in limbo, Prime Minister Jacques Chirac ordered an assault. In two successive attacks, three hundred French troops stormed the cave, firing ten thousand rounds of bullets. Thirteen Kanaky boys and two hostages were killed. Six more Kanaky youths were executed after the attack.

Because of international outrage against the attack, the French government began talks to improve relations. These talks resulted in the Matignon Accord—a referendum promising self-government to the Kanaky people. In 1998, the Noumea Accord was issued, granting independence to New Caledonia by 2018.

GHOST CAVE
Malaysia

Malaysia contains more than one thousand caves, many of which are famous for their magnificent size and beauty. Deer Cave contains the world's largest cave passage, which is almost one and a half miles long and no less than three hundred feet high and wide. The world's largest underground chamber, the Sarawark Chamber, can easily accommodate forty jumbo jets. Both are in Gunung Mulu National Park on the island of Borneo. Caves also play a large role in the economy, culture, and history of Malaysia. Archeologists have found evidence of human occupation in Malaysian caves dating back to 40,000 BC.

The Gomantong Caves are renowned for the swallow-like swiftlets that make their nests in the high chambers of the cave. The nesting material is produced from the bird's saliva and has been harvested for more than one thousand years. This jelly-like substance is boiled to make the famous Bird's Nest Soup. Drinking the soup is said to increase one's sex drive and to cure a number of diseases and illnesses. Nest gatherers must scale the cave walls and climb bamboo poles and ladders to collect this high-priced delicacy. Many gatherers are killed or crippled from falls. Clashes among rival nest gatherers also cause numerous deaths. Another well-known cave is the Ghost Cave of Bau. Discovered by Chinese miners, it is the site of the infamous Chinese massacre.

The city of Bau was established in 1823 after large deposits of gold ore were discovered in the district. The town grew rapidly and became known as the Gold Town of Sarawak. Where there is gold, there are those who want to control it. In 1841, an Englishman by the name of James Brooke was installed as the first white Rajah of Sarawak, having been awarded the title after his role in ending the Civil War between the people and the ruling government.

Prior to Brooke's arrival, the Chinese miners were loosely controlled and, after eighteen years of mining, were quite content with their freedom and way of life. Brooke imposed new taxes, prohibited direct export of gold, and put restrictions on the trading of opium and wine with foreign countries.

Tensions continued to grow between Brooke and the miners. In 1856, Brooke allowed the newly formed Borneo Company to begin mining the gold. This infuriated the miners, and a rebellion against Brooke and his government ensued.

In the early hours of February 19, 1857, six hundred miners attacked the town of Kuching. Brooke narrowly escaped by swimming across the Sarawak River. The town was burned down, and five Europeans were beheaded. Lacking weapons, training, and support from local villages, the rebels retreated to the town of Bau.

Forces loyal to Brooke swiftly descended upon Bau and killed hundreds of rebellious miners. Fearing for their lives, the families of the dead miners escaped to Indonesia or fled to the jungles. Many took sanctuary in nearby Ghost Cave.

On February 25, soldiers found the cave and sealed the entrance with a large bonfire. The flames and smoke efficiently exterminated more than five hundred men, women, and children trapped inside. The dead were left in the cave, and the incident was forgotten.

In the 1930s, explorers were amazed at the find of thousands of human bones scattered throughout the cave. The remains were removed and given a proper burial at a local cemetery. The discovery renewed interest in the cave and the history of the area. Townspeople and community leaders rallied together and began restoration. A brick wall and a door were installed inside the cave, not only to preserve artifacts but also to ensure that the spirits of the dead remained in the cave. Today, the site is a popular tourist attraction. Good fortune is said to come to those who pray to the cave spirits.

RATTLESNAKE CAVE
Oklahoma

Bud Stephens was a hard worker and well-liked by most who met him. Life was good for him and his sixteen-year-old wife. Why he became involved with the likes of Martin Joseph we may never know for sure. Perhaps he needed a little extra money, or maybe he just wanted to treat his new bride to a few special gifts. What we do know is that one night Martin convinced Bud to help him steal a few horses. It was an easy job and a quick way to earn some money. During the heist, Martin killed Bud with a bullet to the head and rode off leaving the body.

Martin headed straight to Bud's home and told the worried wife that her husband had been thrown from his horse and was badly injured. He offered to take her to Bud. She agreed, and they rode off on Martin's horse. When they reached a secluded location in the Arbuckle Mountains of Oklahoma, Joseph raped and murdered her before throwing her body into a deep cave.

Joseph had a weakness for liquor that usually got him into trouble. During a drinking binge, he bragged to a friend about the murders he had committed. The friend told Deputy Marshal J. H. Mershon, who promptly charged Martin Joseph with murder.

Mershon needed more than Joseph's loose lips to convict him. He sent out a posse that found the remains of Bud Stephens. Finding Mrs. Stephens involved a little more work. After days of searching, they found a pit matching Joseph's description. Deputy Marshal John Spencer volunteered to be lowered into the hole to search for the body.

The unmistakable smell of death overwhelmed Spencer as he descended into the depths. At the bottom, a den of rattlesnakes startled him with their ominous warning. In the gloom, he could see the girl's body surrounded by the deadly reptiles. Spencer yelled to the men above who swiftly hauled him up.

Spencer tightened the rope around his waist and gathered his courage for a second descent. Again, he was lowered into the darkness, this time armed with a gun in one hand and a lantern in the other.

A roar of gunfire erupted from the cave as Spencer shot the snakes. When the smoke cleared, Spencer grabbed the body and called to his friends to hoist him up. Mershon now had proof of the crimes, and Martin Joseph was sent to Fort Smith, Arkansas, to await trial in federal court.

Presiding over the court was Judge Isaac C. Parker, who was known throughout the territory as "the hanging Judge." Rape and murder carried a mandatory sentence of death. Judge Parker made sure that those responsible for these crimes received their due reward.

The trial for Martin Joseph lasted five days with a swift verdict of guilty on both counts rendered by the jury. On June 29, 1883, Martin was executed by hanging at the Fort Smith gallows.

In the 1969 western movie *True Grit*, actor John Wayne played the role of Rooster Cogburn, a tough deputy marshal who worked for Judge Parker's court at Fort Smith. In a scene admittedly taken from this story, a young woman falls into a deep cave filled with rattlesnakes and human bones. Hearing her cries for help, Wayne descends into the pit on rope with guns blazing, kills the snakes, and saves the woman from certain death. The movie earned Wayne his first Academy Award for best actor.

FELES CAVE
Lelepa Island

One thousand miles off the coast of Australia, in an area of the South Pacific Ocean known as Melanesia, is a chain of eighty islands called Vanuatu. These volcanic islands are topped with a layer of limestone and contain many underground and underwater solution caves and lava tubes. Some of these caves stretch for miles and have yet to be fully explored. One of the popular tourist attractions on the islands is Feles Cave on Lelepa Island.

King Roymata was a great leader in the early history of the islands (1265 AD) and was known for bringing peace to many of the warring tribes. It is said that Roymata was shot in the neck with a poison dart delivered by his own envious brother. The poison induced a slow, debilitating illness. Roymata was brought to Feles Cave, where he finally died.

In the early 1800s, explorers discovered Sandalwood trees growing on several of the Vanuatu islands. This soft wood was cherished for its aromatic scent. It was also burned as incense and used for making ornate boxes. Demand for this wood exhausted all supplies across much of the Northern Hemisphere. With the discovery of a fresh supply, a wave of traders flocked to Vanuatu. The people of Vanuatu traded the wood for many things they needed. However, as the islanders saw their slow-growing trees begin to disappear, they became more restrictive in the amount that could be taken and the value of the trade.

Tensions increased as unsavory traders often felled trees with disregard to ownership and frequently cheated islanders out of payment. This resulted in violent attacks by both sides, with many a white man rumored to have been the main course for evening dinner. The islanders were viewed as savage beasts who must be exterminated.

In one attack by traders, thirty men, women, and children sought shelter in Feles Cave. In an effort to extract them, wood was piled in front of the entrance and set ablaze. Thick white smoke poured into the cave. Within minutes, many died a suffocating death as they searched in vain for the entrance. Others jumped bravely through the barrier of flames, only to be killed or thrown back into the fire.

Violence overshadowed these islands for years to come. After the Sandalwood trees were depleted, the islanders were taken away and used as laborers on Australian sugar plantations. By the turn of the century, thousands had been slaughtered or were missing, and an entire group of people had been almost completely eliminated.

DEAD MAN CAVE
Maryland

Dead Man Cave, in the northwest corner of Maryland, earned its name from a story passed down by local townspeople. References to the cave as a popular attraction date back to the nineteenth century. It is said to be quite extensive with many unexplored passages. It is also rumored to be the final resting-place of a young man murdered by his older brother.

During the 1860s, a family with two sons lived near the cave. The brothers spent hours exploring the cave together, but they also fought and argued constantly. The youngest was reported to be mentally disabled. One day, he disappeared and was never seen again. The police suspected that he was murdered by his older brother and buried in the cave, which subsequently filled in as a result of heavy flooding. The cave was searched, but no trace of the brother was ever found.

In the 1960s, cavers undertook a project to reopen the cave. Trash was removed from the entrance, and the cave was explored for one hundred and fifty feet before large rocks blocked further exploration. A ten-foot-high waterfall enters the cave at a second entrance. Three narrow passages below the waterfall branch off in separate directions; their full extent is unknown. Perhaps explorers will one day push the full limits of Maryland's most notorious cave, and the mystery surrounding it will be finally put to rest.

CAVE OF DEATH
Mexico

In May 1998, Mexico City police discovered a small cave in a wooded area of Chapultepec Park that was filled with bones, including more than thirty human skulls. Several of the skulls were inscribed with red ink. The cave walls were adorned with the remains of dissected animals, along with a painted image of the devil.

The police were led to the cave after a foot chase of two men who shot at them during a routine patrol of the area. One man was found hiding in the cave and was captured. The suspect told the police they used the secluded cave for a place to rape women, and that the bodies of four women could be found buried in one of the adjacent caves. The caves border the edge of a cemetery. Investigators believe some of the bones may be connected to a recent series of grave robbings.

LOYANG CAVE
Philippines

The territory of the Philippines contains more than seven thousand islands. Early explorers of these islands told of a lush paradise, although it is here that Ferdinand Magellan met his untimely demise. Throughout history, these islands have been troubled by unrest and bloodshed because of tensions between governing nations. Malayan settlers first inhabited the area in the thirteenth century, followed by Islamic, Spanish, Filipino, American, and Japanese occupation. Not until 1946 did the Philippines receive full independence.

The outer islands were notorious pirate haunts. Moro

raiders (Muslim pirates) were feared the most. Cunning and ruthless, the Moros were known for their killing, torture, and enslavement of innocent people. For years, they had resisted all attempts by the Spanish to rule them.

In 1775, Moros invaded Spanish settlements on Catanduanes Island. The towns of Virac and Calolbon were pillaged and burned to the ground. Many villagers escaped the onslaught and ran to the shelter of Loyang Cave. The island offered few places to hide, and the people were quickly found. Most were beaten and killed or taken as slaves. After the attack, the bodies were gathered together and buried in a mass grave in the cave. It is believed that more than sixty people died in the massacre.

DEAD MANS HOLE
Texas

Dead Mans Hole is close to the Colorado River near the town of Marble Falls, Texas. The cave, discovered in 1821, was used as a place to hide the bodies of seventeen Union sympathizers who were captured and hung, including that of pro-union judge John R. Scott. A large oak tree once stood at the edge of the seven-foot-diameter opening; its limbs extended over the pit and made a handy place to tie a hangman's rope. When a hanging was finished, the rope was cut and the body conveniently dropped into the one hundred and fifty-foot pit. Those responsible for the hangings were never found.

After the Civil War, the remains were removed and placed in the Burnet County Courthouse. Three bodies were identified, but the rest mysteriously disappeared.

Today, the hanging tree is gone and the cave is gated to control access. On May 23, 1999, the landowner donated the cave and the surrounding 6.5 acres of land to Burnet County to build a park. A granite historical marker at the site relates the cave's history.

CAVE HOME
China

The Shaanxi Province of northern China has a population of almost forty million. Most of these people live in crude cave dwellings carved out in the sides of cliffs that resemble inner-city row homes. Caves have been used for centuries in this area as an effective means for survival in these rugged mountainous regions. When people are packed so tightly together, they should be mindful of what is stored in their cave.

In the early hours of July 16, 2001, a massive explosion ripped through the village of Mafang. The force of the explosion destroyed or damaged hundreds of cave homes up to three miles away. Villagers dug through the rubble and found seventy dead and eight-five wounded. One survivor said the blast was like sitting next to an erupting volcano.

Three days later, the owner of the illegally stored explosives turned himself in to the police. The villager had been manufacturing the explosives and storing them in a cave owned by his younger brother, who was killed in the blast. Making explosives for nearby quarries is a profitable business. The village was known as a place to buy cheap explosives. Recent crackdowns had done little to deter this illegal and popular activity.

Further investigation revealed that Ma Hongqing, a rival villager, who was in debt and out of work, allegedly tried to steal the illegal cache of explosives. Frustrated by his inability to open the locked gate, he threw a lighted detonator into the cave. He was unaware that the cave contained more than thirty tons of explosives. In August 2001, Hongqing was charged with the crime and may face the death penalty.

BAT CAVE
Thailand

Bat guano is a highly effective organic fertilizer that has been mined from caves around the world for hundreds of years. Guano stays in the soil longer than chemical fertilizers and also inhibits many types of fungus. Collecting this precious dung is hard and messy work that involves all the dangers one might expect when entering a cave . . . and sometimes a few more.

On April 2, 1998, in the steamy jungle of Thailand's Nakhon Ratchasima province, five villagers were killed in an explosion from a homemade grenade as they emerged from the Bat Cave carrying sacks of guano. Their bodies were ripped by shrapnel, and the precious guano was scattered across the jungle floor. Two others were injured in the attack. Since territorial disputes over guano rights are common in this area and result in numerous outbreaks of violence every year, the police suspect that rival guano gatherers are responsible for the crime.

OFNET CAVE
Bavaria

The caves of Europe provide a wealth of knowledge about our ancient past. Many envision prehistoric people living a peaceful co-existence in small communal tribes, migrating with the seasons, drawing on cave walls, and supporting a meager life by hunting and living off the land. Recent discoveries in caves, however, provide new clues about the nature of early humans.

Ofnet Cave in Bavaria contains thirty-eight decapitated skulls thought to be the result of a violent massacre that took place more than eight thousand years ago. Most of the skulls are of women and young children. The victims were bludgeoned to death with stone axes and wooden clubs. Some were hit as many as seven times, with males receiving the most wounds. Several skulls show cut-marks suggesting they were also scalped.

Was prehistoric man, at times, a vicious killer, as this site suggests? What caused these people to brutally murder their fellow humans? Was it a fight for food, a territorial dispute, or was the cave used for a waste pile from cannibalistic pleasures, or maybe a place to store trophies from a good day of hunting? Or perhaps this was the rise of a new breed of humans, one that sought power over the meek and wanted to divide and conquer all in its path—a breed that would eventually refine its weapons of war with exquisite methods of mass destruction and extermination.

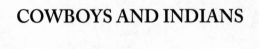

COWBOYS AND INDIANS

DEVILS HOLE
New York

Niagara Falls is on the New York border between Canada and the United States. Its span is the second largest in the world. Twelve million people visit the area every year, yet few know of the tragic events that happened less than four miles downstream.

Prior to the arrival of Europeans, Native Americans of the Iroquois Nation populated much of western New York and the area near Niagara Falls. This nation was an alliance among six tribes, the largest and most powerful of which were the Seneca Indians.

French settlers from Canada and English settlers from the British colonies migrated into the fertile lands of the Iroquois. In the race to claim land, the peaceful existence among the French, the English, and the Iroquois began to erode. After years of small skirmishes, war was finally declared. The French and Indian War lasted six years, resulting in the collapse of the Iroquois Nation. In 1763, Britain declared victory and claimed the land near the falls.

Prior to Britain's victory, the French had employed

the Seneca Indians to help carry supplies along portage routes. Now these routes were controlled by the British, resulting in the Indians' unemployment. The Indians rebelled by attacking important supply routes and outposts. One of the most essential routes for transporting supplies and troops to the Upper Great Lakes region was the Niagara Portage. John Stedman was assigned the job of maintaining this route and keeping it safe.

The most treacherous area of the Niagara Portage was on the American side, three and a half miles downstream from the falls, a place the Indians called "Crawl on All Fours." The trail led along the top of the Niagara River Gorge and crossed an overhanging ledge three hundred feet above the river. Directly below the ledge was a cave the Seneca Indians called Devils Hole.

The entrance was eight feet high and ten feet wide, and the cave extended for three-quarters of a mile. A small stream cascaded over the mouth of the cave. An evil spirit in the form of a giant snake was believed to inhabit the cave, and anyone who disturbed its rest would be murdered. In 1678, French explorer Robert de la Salle ignored the warnings of an Indian guide and entered the cave. Soon after, his exploration of America was plagued with disasters, and he was ultimately murdered. The Indians believed that this was the result of his disturbing the "Evil One."

On the morning of September 14, 1763, a British supply convoy led by John Stedman was returning to Fort Niagara. As they crossed the ledge, the war cries of several hundred Seneca Indians were heard, followed by a fusillade of flaming arrows. Stedman, who was at the front of the wagon train, quickly rode away to summon help from nearby Fort Schlosser. Within moments, the entire convoy was surrounded, and all but two men were brutally massacred. Two companies of British soldiers from Fort Gray arrived to help. They, too, were outnumbered and slaughtered by the Indians.

When troops from Fort Schlosser finally arrived, they found the victims had been scalped and their bodies mutilated. The wagon train, horses, and many of the dead and living had been thrown down into the mouth of Devils Hole. Bodies hung lifeless in the trees below. The small stream ran red with blood and has ever since been called the "Bloody Run." One witness described the stream as a "torrent purple with human gore." Fearing another attack, the soldiers abruptly withdrew to the fort. British troops returned several days later to bury the dead. Commander Sir William Johnson reported that five officers, sixty-four privates, and twenty-one civilians were murdered in the ambush.

On September 13, 1902, the Niagara Frontier Land Marks Association unveiled a plaque at the base of the cliff to commemorate the Devils Hole massacre. Today, Devils Hole State Park encompasses much of this scenic area. It is a popular destination for hikers, fishermen, and ghost hunters.

The cave is believed to be haunted by at least a dozen extremely tormented souls. Visitors to the cave commonly report strange noises coming from its depths. Since 1850, the site has averaged one death a year from murders, suicides, and falls from the sheer cliff walls. According to one guidebook, any attempts to explore the cave would be done at "tremendous personal risk."

KINGSLEY CAVE
California

Lassen Volcanic National Park in northern California covers an area of more than one hundred and fifty square miles. This remote area is characterized by flat ridges, sheer canyon walls, volcanic pillars, deep ravines, and numerous caves. In the southwest portion of the park is the Ishi Wilderness, named after the last survivor of the Yahi Indians.

The Yahi lived in this area undisturbed for three thousand years, but all that changed with the discovery of gold in the creeks and riverbeds of the foothills. As miners and settlers migrated deeper into the mountains, the Yahi were forced from their native lands.

The California gold rush devastated the land and wildlife populations. Forests were cut down, cattle, oxen, and sheep trampled the grasslands, and hydraulic mining polluted the rivers. Hundreds of Yahi died from hunger, disease, and forced migration. But without question, most were killed by mass-slaughter. In just over twenty years, the Yahi Indians of this region were systematically eliminated. By 1871, only a few groups were still hiding in the deep canyons. What is believed to be the final massacre of the tribe, the Kingsley Cave Massacre, occurred in April 1871.

Norman Kingsley and three other men were searching the hills for stray cattle when they found a trail of blood that led to a gutted steer stripped of its meat. A broken arrow was also nearby. The men returned the following day with dogs and continued the search for the killers of the steer. The dogs led them along the banks of Mill Creek to the mouth of a large cave.

From the opposite side of a narrow gulch, the four

men could see more than thirty Yahi Indians in the cave. Without a second thought, the men fired into the cave and slaughtered the helpless Indians. Norman Kingsley later said that he changed from his .56-caliber Spencer rifle to a .38-caliber Smith and Wesson revolver because the rifle "tore them up so bad," particularly the babies. This cave was believed to be the last stronghold of the now exterminated Yahi Indians—a tribe whose peaceful existence was shattered by greed, prejudice, and the rush of gold fever.

On August 29, 1911, a lone Yahi Indian walked out of the hills and into the White Man's world. Ishi had survived, along with his mother and a few others, undetected for forty years in the rugged terrain of Dear Creek Canyon. After the last of his people died, Ishi chose not to live alone. In a desperate act of survival, dazed and half-starved, he entered the modern world. For the next five years, he lived under the care and protection of Alfred Kroeber at the University of California.

On March 24, 1916, Ishi died of tuberculosis. His remains were cremated and his brain sent to the Smithsonian Museum of Natural History, where it was placed in storage for the next eighty-three years. In August 2000, his brain was returned to a close relation of the Yahi tribe and buried in an undisclosed location in Deer Creek Canyon.

MASSACRE CAVE
Arizona

Native Americans have inhabited the southwest region of Arizona known as Canyon de Chelly for almost two thousand years. The abundance of plants and animals, along with the protection the canyons offered, made this area well-suited for living. Within the canyon walls, rims, and bottomlands, many prehistoric artifacts and rock drawings are preserved. In 1931, President Herbert Hoover designated one hundred and thirty square miles of this area as a national monument to protect this archeological sanctuary.

The Anasazi Indians were among the first people to live in this area. After the Anasazi disappeared, the Hopi and Pueblo Indians settled in the canyon lands. Around 1700, the Navajo Indians moved into Canyon de Chelly, driving out the Pueblo Indians.

As Spanish settlers from New Mexico began to move into Navajo territory, frequent conflicts resulted between the two. For years, ranchers and the Spanish army fought against the Navajo. Each blamed the other when cattle and sheep disappeared. During the winter of 1804–05, under the direction of Lieutenant Colonel Antonio Narbona, the Spanish army mounted a punitive expedition to teach the Navajo a lesson once and for all.

The Navajo had played this game before and sought shelter in a cave nearly one thousand feet up the canyon wall. This site had offered ample protection in the past when their pursuers fought with rocks and bows and arrows, but the Spaniards were using a new weapon: the accurate long-barreled musket.

After finding the Indians, Narbona sent a group of men to the high rim of the opposite canyon where they could see directly down into the cave. Another group was sent to the canyon floor to eliminate all possibilities of escape. The sounds of guns echoed for hours as the men fired into the cave.

When the guns fell silent, one hundred and fifteen men, women, and children lay massacred in a bloody heap. Ninety male warriors were killed. Thirty-three Indians survived the massacre and were taken into slavery. One old Indian was left for dead but survived to tell of the horrors from that day. Narbona himself mutilated the bodies and cut off the ears of eighty-four warriors as trophies.

Only one Spaniard was killed during the battle. He was the first to enter the cave and was attacked by a Navajo woman. During the scuffle, they both fell to the canyon floor. The Navajo call this cave *"ah tah ho do nilly"* meaning "two fell off." Bones littered the cave and the canyon floor until they were eventually buried years later.

This is one of the most sacred sites for the Navajo Indians, who believe it is haunted by the spirits of the dead. Today, it is commonly called Massacre Cave, and the cave walls still bear the scars from that day.

APACHE DEATH CAVE
Arizona

The ghost town of Two Guns, Arizona, is thirty miles east of Flagstaff along legendary Route 66. This once bustling tourist trap offered the weary traveler gas, food, Indian ruins, a roadside zoo, and overnight accommodations.

Today, this Route 66 icon lies in shambles. A fence surrounds the property in an attempt to preserve the crumbling structures. An armed caretaker lives on the premises and will provide a personal tour of the town for $5.00. One of the popular attractions of Two Guns is the Apache Death Cave, also called the Cave of Death. The cave is approximately one hundred and twenty feet long and is part of the Earthcrack System that extends across Arizona.

Many confrontations between Navajo and Apache Indians took place in this area. The Apaches raided Navajo camps to steal food, horses, and Navajo women. The raiding parties then escaped into Canyon Diablo, where they disappeared.

During a raid in 1878, Navajo braves chased the raiding Apaches into the canyon and cornered them in a cave. The Navajos then gathered wood and brush and built a large fire at the entrance. Any Apaches who tried to escape were attacked and killed. Those who remained in the cave faced a volley of arrows and bullets as thickening smoke billowed into the cave.

In a desperate act of survival, the Apaches tried to put out the flames with their horses' blood. Some Apaches crawled inside their gutted horses to escape the heat and smoke. When the fire burned out, the charred remains of forty-two Apaches were left to rot on the blackened cave floor.

During the construction of Route 66, the bones and skulls were removed from the cave and placed on fence posts along the road to attract tourists. A purchase from the nearby trading post allowed the buyer the choice of a bone from the exhibit. Today, there is an Apache shrine in the cave to honor the dead. Although the bones are long gone, it is believed that evil spirits will curse anyone who disturbs the cave.

DEVILS CAVE
Illinois

Devils Cave, also called Coon Den Cave, is in northeastern Illinois along the south bank of the Fox River. In the 1820s, this was the land of the Potawatomi Indians. These peaceful Indians spent the summer living in villages along the river. During the winter months, they migrated south but returned each spring to the fertile lands of the Fox River Valley. One of the great leaders of the tribe was Chief Waubonsie, whose village was opposite the cave. The Potawatomi never lived in the cave, but its inviting entrance and three hundred feet of passage became a sordid part of the tribe's history.

Chief Waubonsie was a great warrior for much of his life, but he had learned there was nothing to be gained from war or bloodshed. The younger Indians of the village did not understand his talk of peace. Fueled by stories of their fathers and grandfathers, they knew an Indian was judged by how strong and brave a warrior he was.

Following the traditions of the past, many of the young braves would ride out on their horses and return several days later with plunder they had stolen from nearby settlers. As complaints from settlers increased, the United States government gave harsh warnings to all the tribes who engaged in these crimes. Waubonsie told his men that these raids would no longer be tolerated and that they were to end their raids or face banishment from the tribe.

Days after the warning, a young Indian rode proudly into the village with clothing and food taken during his lone raid on newly arrived settlers. The warrior was brought before a tribal council and banished from the tribe. The wayward Indian headed north to join the Winnebago Indians, and all was forgotten by early summer.

In the fall, a frightening and evil presence was seen on the darkest nights walking through the woods and along the riverbanks. This apparition had a human form but glowed as if on fire. The ghostly specter appeared and disappeared into thin air.

Shortly after the first sighting of the "Evil Spirit," several Indians from Waubonsie's tribe were murdered and scalped, and a young squaw was killed while picking berries. They also found the scalped bodies of a hunter and a fisherman. The medicine man convinced the tribe that a spirit of the dead, or perhaps even the Devil himself, was responsible for these crimes.

The man of fire terrorized the tribe for weeks. However, when the Indians discovered that this spirit left footprints similar to their own, they became less fearful and decided it was time to hunt it down. On the next moonless night, several Indians hid in the woods and waited for the spirit to return. As soon as they saw it, the Indians took chase. The glowing man ran into the cave and vanished.

Why would a spirit run away? The Indians were now convinced that this was the work of a man, perhaps a settler trying to scare them. Knowing it was now trapped inside the cave, they decided to smoke it out. Waubonsie and his men swiftly gathered wood and brush, and built a huge fire that engulfed the entrance. Through the smoke a figure wrapped in a blanket ran from the cave and plunged into the river.

By morning's light, a body was found washed up on the river's edge. When the blanket was removed it was revealed their Evil Spirit was really the young brave who was banished from the tribe months ago. His body was smeared with foxfire—a glowing fungus produced from decaying wood. By covering and uncovering himself with the blanket he could make his glowing body appear and disappear.

From that day the cave was called the Cave of the Evil Spirit or, as it is known today, Devils Cave. Some believe the ghost of the young brave still haunts the area. On dark nights, his glowing body is sometimes seen walking along the river.

QUEHO CAVE
Arizona

Stories of the Wild West are full of colorful figures who have been immortalized in books and movies and have shaped our vision of the American frontier. It was a lawless place where the fastest gun ruled the land.

In 1880, an Indian boy named Queho (pronounced Kway-ho) was born near Las Vegas, Nevada. His mother died shortly after giving birth, and the identity of his father was never known. This was at the height of the Indian wars, and a dangerous time to be an Indian. General Custer already had his Last Stand, and the great Indian Chiefs Sitting Bull, Geronimo, and Wounded Knee had yet to surrender.

Queho was raised on a reservation near Las Vegas. Early in his youth it was apparent he was a troubled child. A birth defect of a clubfoot added to his misery and his withdrawal from society. From the confines of the reservation, Queho became Nevada's first mass murderer and Public Enemy Number One.

In 1910, Queho committed his first known crime: the

murder of a crazy Paiute Indian named Harry Bismark. Harry was not well liked and having one less Indian in town did not seem to bother anyone. Queho's next victim was J. M. Woodworth; a white man whose skull he bashed in with a piece of lumber. Killing an Indian was one thing, but killing a white man was something entirely different. Queho fled into the hills with an angry posse hot on his trail.

Queho crossed over the Colorado River into Arizona and continued his killing spree. Doc Gilbert, the night watchman of the Gold Bug Mine, was found dead with a bullet in his head. The guard's food was stolen and his Special Deputy badge #896 was missing. Trackers found Queho's unmistakable footprints at the scene and continued their pursuit into the hills and valleys that bordered the Colorado River. Following an Indian with a bad foot, they thought, would be an easy task, but Queho proved to be an elusive quarry.

To the embarrassment of law officers, and despite a large "Dead or Alive" reward, Queho successfully evaded capture. To the Indians, he was a hero; to the white man, he was just another crazy Indian. Sightings of him continued for years, and any unsolved crime or murder was blamed on the rebel Indian. Twenty-three killings were credited to him.

On February 18, 1940, two prospectors discovered a cave high up a canyon wall along the Nevada side of the Colorado River. A low stone wall concealed the entrance, and a tripwire tied to a bell gave warning of approaching guests. Inside the cave, they found the remains of an American Indian. They also found several loaded guns, clothing, food, a bow and arrows, strings of wampum, and a Special Deputy badge #896.

The following day, the prospectors returned to the

cave with the county coroner and Las Vegas Chief of Police Frank Wait, who identified the remains as the long sought-after Indian. Frank Wait had been one of the original members of the 1910 posse seeking Queho. It was determined that Queho died of natural causes approximately six months prior to being found.

The remains were removed from the cave and given to a local funeral parlor, but the saga was far from over. For the next three years, a battle raged in the courts over legal custody of the body, who should get the items found and the reward money, and who would pay the funeral parlor embalming and storage expenses. To complicate matters, several Indians claimed to be relatives of Queho, and they, too, wanted their share. After all the squabbling, Frank Wait paid the bills and took everything. In a bizarre twist, Wait gave the body and items to the Las Vegas Elks Club. Burying Queho was simply out of the question.

The Elks built a full-size replica of the cave and placed Queho and his belongings in it for public display, creating a popular tourist attraction for anyone traveling through town. Thus, in death Queho was mistreated and abused. By the mid-1960s, interest in Queho diminished, and the display was removed. The remains were then owned by several people and finally by the Museum of Natural History, until they were properly laid to rest on November 6, 1975. The items found with the body have disappeared.

The spirit of Queho is said to haunt the area of the cave. To this day, mysterious disappearances near Las Vegas are still blamed on Nevada's most infamous Indian.

BETTY MOODY CAVE
New Hampshire

S ix miles off the coast of New Hampshire are nine islands called Isles of the Shoals. They were first inhabited by the English in the seventeenth century and became a haven for fishermen, smugglers, and marauding pirates. Rumors abound of buried treasure. Blackbeard's hoard of ill-gotten gold is believed to be hidden somewhere on these islands.

Star Island is the only island in the chain accommodated by ferry service, and it is today a popular destination for tourists and corporate conferences. Historic tours of Star Island are popular among sightseers. One of the attractions is Betty Moody Cave.

During the King Philip War (1675–77), skirmishes with the Wampanoag Indians were common on the islands. In one raid, Indian warriors, confident the men were out to sea fishing, sailed to Star Island and attacked. House by house, the Indians terrorized the islanders. Fearing for her life and the lives of her two children, Betty Moody fled to a small, damp cave at the water's edge.

In the cave, her youngest child was inconsolable. The baby cried continuously, terrified by the darkness and the shrill screams of nearby Indians. Knowing that capture, torture, and most assuredly death awaited them if found, Betty silenced her child by the only means possible. In an act of mad terror, she strangled her baby to death. For the moment all was silent, and Betty took solace in knowing she had at least saved her remaining child's life.

Her comfort was short-lived. An Indian appeared at the entrance and dragged Betty and her older child from the cave. Along the shore, she broke free from his grasp. In one last desperate act, she flung herself and her child into the waves, never to be seen again. This area of the beach is known today as Betty Moody Cove. Locals have reported seeing the ghost of Betty Moody and her two children walking along the shoreline. Others have reported hearing a baby's cry and of feeling a strange presence inside the cave.

SKELETON CAVE
Arizona

In 1863, the discovery of gold in Arizona drove miners and farmers deeper into its western reaches. This was the territory of the Yavapai Indians. Early Spanish explorers described the Yavapai as peaceful Indians who led a nomadic existence by moving across Arizona in small groups.

Within a few years, the Yavapai found themselves and their hunting grounds in the path of the settlers' growth. Tensions grew as skirmishes between the Yavapai and the settlers increased. Complaints about the hostile Indians forced the United States Army to place a military outpost at Verde River in 1865. In the aftermath of the American Civil War, soldiers had found a new enemy to fight: the American Indian.

As the conflicts increased across the region, the government established the Rio Verde Reservation in 1871 under the command of Lieutenant Colonel George Crook. Crook's job was to bring peace to the region and put an end to the raids. He ordered that any Yavapai Indians found off the reservation were to be treated as hostile and shot on sight.

By 1872, most of the Yavapai had surrendered, but

within the Superstition Mountains small groups continued to resist. Apache scouts working for the army knew of an isolated cave deep in the mountains along the Salt River Canyon that raiders were using as a refuge. Under the direction of Major William H. Brown, two hundred and twenty soldiers from the Fifth Cavalry set out in search of the cave.

On December 28, 1872, Brown's soldiers found the cave and the Indians hidden in a steep canyon wall seven hundred feet above the Salt River. One group of soldiers descended from the mesa to surround the cave. Another group stayed on top to guard against an attack from the rear. The soldiers opened fire as the first rays of sunlight entered the cave. From above, soldiers dropped cannon-ball-sized boulders that triggered a huge rockfall into the cave.

When the shooting stopped and the smoke cleared, more than one hundred men, women, and children lay massacred. The few who survived were either killed or taken away by the soldiers. The bodies of the dead were left in the cave.

From that day forward, the cave was called Skeleton Cave or Skull Cave, and the massacre was remembered as the most horrible event in Yavapai history. Captain John G. Bourke, who took part in the massacre, wrote: "Never have I seen such a hellish spot as was the narrow little space in which the hostile Indians were now crowded."

After the massacre, the resistance and spirit of the Yavapai was broken. They now knew that their most hidden retreats could be found. The remaining Indians surrendered and settled into the Rio Verde Reservation.

SKULL CAVE
Mackinac Island

Mackinac Island is a secluded isle in the waters of Lake Huron and lies seven miles from the mainland of Michigan. A trip to the island is like stepping back in time. The island is accessible only by boat, and the only forms of transportation permitted are bicycles and horses. Tourists not only flock to the island for its elegance and charm but also to experience a long-lost way of life in this authentic Victorian setting.

Life was not always grand here. A considerable amount of bloodshed has occurred on the island from decades of fighting among the French and British Armies, American Colonies, and Native Americans.

In 1763, more than three hundred and fifty of Chief Pontiac's braves attacked Fort Michilimackinac on the Michigan coast. They murdered ninety-three English soldiers before being driven off. During the battle, Alexander Henry, an English fur trader, was taken prisoner.

For days, Alexander was tormented and moved from place to place. Fearing an attack by the English, his captors moved him by canoe to what was then called Michilimackinac Island. As luck would have it, Alexander was found by Wawatum, a Chippewa Indian who years before had adopted Alexander as his brother. Wawatum convinced the tribe to spare Alexander's life, but he still feared for Alexander's security. When the braves, who had seized a large quantity of liquor, began drinking heavily, he hid Alexander in a small remote cave and promised to return when all was safe.

Alexander spent a sleepless night trying to stay comfortable in the cold and rocky cave. As the morning light crept into the cave, Alexander viewed his surroundings.

With awakening horror, he realized that the rocks and branches on which he has so desperately tried to sleep were actually human skulls and bones. Wawatum returned to the cave two days later and, with Alexander disguised as a brave, helped him safely off the island. The cave has come to be known as Skull Cave, Skull Rock, or Cave of the Skulls.

Opinions differ as to how the bones came to be in the cave. One belief is that a group of Indians who were hiding from a rival tribe, had taken refuge there but had been found and massacred with a large fire built at the entrance. Another idea is that the cave was used as a burial cave. Still others believe that, during a flood of the island, Indians sought shelter in the cave and drowned.

Today, a sign outside the cave tells about Alexander and his troubled night's stay. The bones have long since been buried, and much of the cave has been destroyed. People still come to see this popular tourist attraction and to envision the thoughts poor Alexander Henry must have had as he awoke in an underground grave.

MASSACRE ISLAND CAVE
Canada

Massacre Island is on the Saint Lawrence River, near the town of Bic, Canada. In 1533, approximately two hundred Micmac Indians were camped on the island when a rival party of Iroquois were seen coming ashore. The Micmacs ran to the shelter of a cave and concealed the entrance with brush. They had used this refuge many times in the past.

The Iroquois searched the island until they found the Micmacs. When the Indians refused to come out, the entrance brush was set ablaze, filling the small cave with deadly smoke. Those who were lucky enough to escape the flames and smoke were brought down with arrows and tomahawks. Only five Micmacs survived the massacre.

French explorer Jacques Cartier, who explored this area while searching for a passage through North America, wrote in his journals about the massacre as told to him by the Indians. Recently a cave was found on an island in the Saint Lawrence River that contained a large number of human bones, giving added credence to the account.

THE SPOILS OF WAR

ARDEATINE CAVES
Rome

On January 22, 1944, Allied troops landed on the beaches of Anzio, Italy, with the goal of liberating the German-occupied city of Rome. The Eternal City is less than forty miles from the beachhead, yet it took almost six months of fierce fighting before Allied troops finally entered Rome.

Inside the city, German troops were weakening because of the persistent underground movement against them. One of the strongest partisan groups was the communist Front for Patriotic Action, the Gruppi di Azione Patriottica (GAP). GAPists were responsible for daily attacks and bombings that caused many casualties among the German soldiers. Although the Germans did not take this harassment lightly, they had not yet taken any action against it. Soon, however, that would change with horrifying consequences.

On the afternoon of March 23, 1944, a column of one hundred and fifty-six German police, escorted by armored vehicles, made their daily parade through Rome up the narrow street of Via Rasella. The rhythmic sound of their marching feet and their loud singing announced the troops' arrival. As the Germans approached, Rosario Bentivegna, a GAP member disguised as a street cleaner lit the fuse of a forty-pound bomb hidden in a rubbish cart. The bomb was encased in steel and packed with small pieces of iron. At 3:34 p.m., the bomb exploded and ripped the German column to shreds. The huge explosion was heard throughout the center of Rome. Three more explosions followed from grenades tossed at soldiers.

Twenty-six soldiers were instantly killed, and more than seventy were wounded. This was the most serious attack yet by the partisans. Lieutenant-General Kurt Maeltzer, the German Commandant in Rome, threatened to blow up the entire street, and many residents were pulled out of their homes and beaten.

Hitler was enraged at the news of the attack and demanded that the entire area near Via Rasella be burned and all the inhabitants shot. He later changed the order: within twenty-four hours he now wanted ten Italians executed for each of the thirty-three Germans killed.

The job of finding three hundred and thirty people to execute was delegated to the Security Service of Hitler's elite Secret State Police. They started in the prisons. Any prisoners condemned to die or to serve long terms of hard labor were taken, along with those who had committed crimes the Germans felt warranted the death penalty. Still, they came up short of the required head count. In a rush to meet the twenty-four-hour deadline, they added seventy-five Jews to the list, including ten people from the street of Via Rasella. Now that they had their victims, the next questions were where, how, and who was going to kill these people? And what were they to do with the bodies afterwards?

The ideal place was soon found. A quarry outside town contained several caves with a network of intersecting passages, some of which were three hundred feet long, ten feet wide, and more than fifteen feet high. The caves had been excavated forty years earlier for sand used to make concrete. Locals called them the Ardeatine Caves. Here the prisoners could be killed and buried all in one place.

The officers decided that the Gestapo, under the direction of Lieutenant-Colonel Herbert Kappler, would execute the prisoners. Anyone who did not follow orders would also be shot. The prisoners were loaded into meat trucks under heavy guard and driven to the caves. Until then, they had been unsure about their destination or the reason for their movement. Now their fate was certain.

The prisoners were tied together in groups of five and marched into the cave. The passages were lit with torches held by soldiers. At the end of the farthest tunnel, the prisoners were ordered to kneel down, and each was shot at the base of the skull with a single bullet.

As the killings continued, it became apparent that the line of dead bodies would soon reach the entrance. To save room, prisoners were ordered to climb on top of the dead before being shot. Soldiers, too, had to climb the carnal heap to reach their victims.

The stress of killing so many innocent people had an adverse effect on Kappler's seventy-four-man execution team. A rest period was called, and the men were ordered to get drunk. This helped ease the pain of killing, but it also made the soldiers' work sloppy. At times, several shots were needed to kill a man. Others were killed with rifle butts, and still others were left to die amidst the growing pile of bodies.

At 8:00 p.m., the executions ended, and a battalion

of German engineers closed the cave entrance with explosives. Five extra victims were killed in error, bringing the total to three hundred and thirty-five dead. Although the area was heavily guarded, there were witnesses to the killings, and word of the crime rapidly spread throughout Rome. A priest discovered a way into one of the caves and told of the horrors he had found. Within days, an incredible stench permeated the area. To mask the smell, soldiers dumped garbage at the entrance of the caves, but this still did not hide the terrible odor. German engineers then sealed the caves completely with several large explosions.

On June 4, 1944, American troops entered Rome, liberating the city. Almost immediately, the exhumation of the bodies from the caves began. Day after day, townspeople dug through the rubble to look for loved ones. The war ended nine months later, but the memory of the worst Nazi atrocity in Italy would never be forgotten.

In 1948, an Italian court found Lieutenant-Colonel Herbert Kappler guilty of war crimes and sentenced him to life in prison. In 1977, he escaped from a prison hospital in Rome and fled to western Germany, where he died of stomach cancer the following year.

Every year since 1944, many Romans make a pilgrimage to the Ardeatine Caves in remembrance of that day. The area is now a national memorial with a mausoleum that contains the remains of the victims in three hundred and thirty-five marble coffins.

KOCEVSKI ROG CAVES
Slovenia

Slovenia, located in southern Europe along the Adriatic Sea and bordered by Austria, Italy, Croatia, and Hungary, is approximately the size of New Jersey. Two-thirds of Slovenia consists of limestone, and almost half of its territory is classified as karst area. More than 7,800 caves have been discovered in this small country.

The Kras region of Slovenia is where the word "karst" originated and where the first research of karst morphology and hydrology took place. The famous Postojna Cave is in Slovenia, along with Vilenica Cave, the oldest tourist cave in the world. One area rich in caves is the dense forest region of Kocevski Rog. Many of the caves in this high karst massif are large open pits up to thirty feet across and more than three hundred feet deep. Although many of these caves remain unexplored, the grim reality of what may be found in them is without question.

In the waning days of World War II, the partisan armies of Marshal Josip Broz (Tito) had the German and Croatian armies retreating north, across Slovenana, toward the Austrian border. Tito became the leader of the partisan resistance after Germany invaded Yugoslavia in 1941. His guerilla armies had fought hard and had proved to be a formidable force. By 1945, much of Slovenia, then a part of Yugoslavia, was liberated and controlled by Tito's communist fighters.

On May 15, 1945, ten days after the war's end, more than 160,000 Balkan refugees and Croatian soldiers entered the small town of Bleiburg, Austria, and surrendered to the British with a promise they would not be returned to Yugoslavia and the partisans. Unknown to these people, the trains they boarded were not taking them to prisoner-of-war camps in Italy but back across the border into the legal custody of Tito's armies. This turn of events is known as the Bleiburg Tragedy and is one of the world's greatest military betrayals. Within days, tens of thousands were slaughtered. Others were bound and marched hundreds of miles to remote sites, the way littered with bodies and mass graves. The isolated forests and the deep caves of Kocevski Rog proved to be the perfect killing fields.

During the first days of June 1945, men, women, and children were marched to the edge of the deep pits and ravines, where they were shot and then tossed into the pits. Others were thrown in alive, but not before they were stripped of useful clothing, gold teeth removed with gunstocks, and women raped. As the pits filled, they were topped with rock and soil. To save ammunition, the prisoners were tied together in groups of six and forced to walk on planks placed across the pits. The closest prisoner was then hit on the head, forcing the entire group to fall into the black abyss. Only four men escaped death by climbing out of the pits at night before they were sealed.

Hundreds of trucks packed with prisoners passed through the small towns but returned only with loads of bundled clothing. For weeks, locals heard screams and gunshots coming from the forests. One witness said the dirt that covered the pits would move and rise as the thousands of rotting bodies swelled the fresh soil. Bulldozers were constantly used to repack the tainted earth. Some estimate that more than thirty thousand people are buried in the caves of Kocevski Rog, with more than half a million killed in all.

Today, the landscape tells its own grim tale. In the gloom of a dense forest canopy, mourners have placed crosses and rosary beads at cave entrances. Sinkholes also mark the locations of the pits. Several have opened to expose bone and leather clothing.

The caves, too, tell their own tale of a country torn by war and revolution. German soldiers once used the large entrance room of Postojna Cave to store petrol, oil, and ammunition. With guards at the entrance, the Germans felt sure their supplies were protected from enemy intrusion. They never expected raiders to enter through a connection from another cave. Behind the backs of the Germans, partisans set fire to hundreds of barrels of fuel that burned for a week. Black soot still covers the walls and ceiling.

In 1990, another one of Tito's massacre sites was found in Sosice, Yugoslavia. Jazovka Cave may contain the remains of thousands. Villagers have always known about the site but were afraid to speak of it. Across Slovenia, human remains have been found in eighty-six caves.

CAVE OF THE CRYING STREAM
South Korea

In the early hours of June 25, 1950, seventy thousand North Korean soldiers invaded South Korea, thus beginning the Korean War. Seoul, the capital of South Korea, fell to North Korea in four days. On September 15, 1950, American forces under the command of General MacArthur landed in Inchon and successfully took control of Seoul. North Korean troops occupied the capital three more times by the war's end.

The war left mass destruction in its wake for cities such as Seoul and others along both sides of the border. Roads were lined with millions of Koreans fleeing the towns in search of food and shelter, and the safety of refugee camps. North Korean soldiers disguised in common white civilian clothing were among the refugees fleeing into South Korea. For American pilots, it was increasingly difficult to distinguish between refugees and the enemy. Fighter pilots depended on controller planes to direct them to their targets. Many attacks were carried out on people dressed in white clothing. Whether they were soldiers was uncertain at times.

One such incident happened at the Cave of the Crying Stream. The cave, located in South Korea near the town of Youngchoon, is four hundred feet long and is named for the sound it makes as floodwaters pour from its entrance.

As North Korean and Chinese troops pushed farther into South Korea, thousands of refugees poured into the town of Youngchoo. The large cave outside the town became a natural shelter for hundreds of people huddled together with their belongings. Straw mats were spread across the damp floor, and kerosene lamps were used to light the cave.

According to witnesses, on January 20, 1951, an observer plane circled overhead several times. Then four American jets swooped down to drop incendiary bombs and to spray the area with machine-gun fire. The entrance exploded in flames that spread throughout the cave and killed more than three hundred refugees.

In the succeeding days, survivors picked through the pile of bodies looking for loved ones. Most of the dead were left in the cave and were never identified. Years after the attack, skeletal remains continued to float out of the cave during floods. The ancients who named the cave had no idea how fitting a name it was.

DEVILS DEN
Pennsylvania

In the summer of 1863, having failed in his first attempt to invade northern soil, General Robert E. Lee moved his troops across the Potomac River and into the peaceful countryside of Pennsylvania. At the small farming town of Gettysburg, Lee's troops met Union troops under the command of General George G. Meade. For the next three days, both sides fought the bloodiest and most decisive battle of the Civil War.

Especially fierce fighting took place in an area known as Devils Den. This large upheaval of igneous rock is several thousand feet long and up to thirty feet tall. The rocks contain several talus caves up to sixty feet long and a small stream called Plum Run.

As the two lines of armies approached each other, Devils Den was on their flank. Both sides knew that controlling this position could help win the battle. Both Union and Confederate sharpshooters were positioned in the cracks and crevices of these rocks and skillfully cut down the approaching enemy. The caves also served as a shelter for the wounded, a place to find water, and a temporary escape from battle. These rocks were also deathtraps as bullets and shells splintered and ricocheted about.

Devils Den changed hands several times during the fighting. By the third day, the rocks were stained with blood, and the water of Plum Run ran red. After the battle, more than one hundred bodies lay within the jumble of rocks and caves.

The great battle claimed more than fifty thousand dead and wounded. Curious sightseers drawn to Devils Den said that the stench of the dead lingered for months and that bleached white bones lay everywhere. This area is still one of the most popular Civil War tourist attractions. People not only come to admire the beautiful Pennsylvania landscape but also to step back in time to a place of man and war.

Gettysburg is believed to be one of the most haunted sites in the country. Stories persist of moans coming from the caves, sightings of ghosts dressed in Civil War era clothing, sounds of battle, and problems with electrical equipment in and near the area of Devils Den.

CAVE OF LETTERS
Israel

The Judean Desert in Israel is one of the most desolate and barren places on Earth. Midday temperatures can reach one hundred and twenty degrees during the summer months. Along its western border, mountains rise from the shores of the Dead Sea to form a moonscape-like setting.

For thousands of years people have sought refuge in the hundreds of caves that pockmark the valleys of this region, and they have left behind a horde of valuable records and artifacts. In 1947, the Dead Sea Scrolls were found in caves within this area, a discovery that prompted treasure hunters to start searching every corner of the desert. In 1951, Bedouins discovered a cave six hundred feet above the valley floor in the Wadi Murabba'at Canyon. The cave contained bronze objects and ancient letters written by Simon Bar-Kokhba to his commanders.

Simon Bar-Kokhba was a legendary hero of the Jewish people and the leader of the Second Jewish Revolt against Rome (132–135 AD), but little was actually known about his life. The letters revealed him to be a tough man and a smart warrior. Although the Jewish people fought hard for three years to reestablish Judea as a Jewish state, they were no match for the armies of the Roman Empire. After the war, Jerusalem was rebuilt as a Roman colony, with Jews forbidden to enter. With their belongings, Jewish refugees fled to the mountains and caves of the Judean wilderness.

In 1953, Israel's Department of Antiquities assembled a team of archeologists to investigate what is now called the Cave of Letters. The team found that the Bedouins had ransacked and littered the cave. One member of the team squeezed through a narrow opening, where he discovered a clothed human skeleton pinned under a rock. Clothing samples proved that the cave was occupied during the Bar-Kokhba era. To the disappointment of the group, little more was found there.

In the following years, more Hebrew texts appeared on the antiquities market. All were discovered in the caves that bordered the Dead Sea. Annoyed by the looting of their caves, Israel again sent teams of archeologists to scour the southern Judean area. The most significant finds came from the most unlikely place: the Cave of Letters.

Using military mine detectors, archeologists found a treasure trove of bronze vases, bowls, jugs, jewelry, and coins buried in the cave floor. One man squeezed past a constriction to discover a small room and a ghastly sight. Along the wall were baskets filled with human skulls, and the floor was littered with bones and clothing. The grim reality of what happened to the cave's prior occupants was revealed.

These were the remains of seventeen Bar-Kokhba warriors and their families who were forced into the desert by advancing troops. The Romans must have known that they had trapped important people. The cave was accessible only from the plateau where the Romans camped to wait them out. The Jews refused to surrender and died a slow death from starvation. Later, unknown people collected the remains and buried them deeper in the cave.

Roman camps were also found above other caves in the area. One cave is called the Cave of Horrors because of the number of skulls and bones it contained. Ancient Jewish sources recount the details of trapped families who were deprived of food and water and were forced to eat the flesh of the dead to survive.

In 1999 and 2000, expeditions returned to the Cave of Letters equipped with ground penetrating radar, endoscopes, and sensitive metal detectors. Using this high-tech equipment, researchers continue to find clues that add to the understanding of the cave and the people who lived and died in it.

MELIDONI CAVE
Crete

Crete, the fifth largest island in the Mediterranean Sea, is midway between the continents of Europe and Africa. This narrow island was once believed to be the center of the world. Habitation of Crete dates back to 3000 BC, and it is considered to be the home of Europe's earliest civilization. More than three thousand caves have been found on Crete, and many still remain unexplored. These caves have been used for places of worship, shelters, and shrines for many of the Greek gods.

One of the most notable caves is Melidoni Cave or Gerontospilios (Old Mans Cave), near the small village of Melidoni. The cave contains four large rooms and several interconnecting passages totaling eight hundred feet in length.

The cave is the mythical home of Talos, the bronze giant who circled the island twice a day guarding the shores. A plaque inside the cave designates it as a sanctuary to the Greek god Hermes. However, for all its fame, Melidoni Cave is most noted in Greek history as a place of unspeakable horror at the hands of the ruling Turks.

Turkish occupation of Crete began in 1669 and lasted for more than two hundred years. Before the Turkish invasion, the people of Crete endured numerous conquerors including Greeks, Romans, Saracens, and Venetians. The era of Turkish rule is a dark period in the history of Crete, marked by nine revolutions. Villages were devastated and thousands of lives lost across every inch of Cretan soil in the fight for freedom and national sovereignty.

By 1824, the Turks dominance on the island was weakening. This resulted in some of the most brutal massacres the people of Crete had ever experienced. In one attack, approximately four hundred refugees consisting of mostly women and children sought shelter in Melidoni Cave. Their location was unfortunately discovered, but the Cretans refused to surrender and leave the protection the cave offered. In an attempt to drive them out, the Turks set timber and brush ablaze and threw it into the cave. The huge entrance room, known today as the Hero's Chamber, roared with flames and smoke. Within minutes all inside were dead. The entrance was then sealed.

The cave was reopened years later, and the remains were interred in a large communal tomb in the cave. Fine black soot from the fire still covers the ceiling and the beautiful formations that adorn the cave.

In 1898, Crete was declared an autonomous state, finally liberated from oppressive Turkish rule. But in 1941, Crete again was threatened. Hitler's armies were ravaging the island and its people. The Germans also used the cave as a convenient place to kill those who opposed their presence. A small memorial dedicated to those victims was erected in the cave. Today, people still visit the area to see a cave torn by war and hatred and to pray in the dark and quiet confines of its hallowed rooms.

CAVE OF THE SLAUGHTER
Arranmore Island

Arranmore Island, three miles off the western coast of Ireland, has been inhabited since 800 BC and boasts a current population of about eight hundred. Its rugged cliffs, sandy beaches, and numerous pubs are popular destinations for tourists and fishermen.

During the mid-1600s the armies of Oliver Cromwell raged across Ireland in an effort to place it under English rule. His troops massacred thousands and devastated town after town. Those who lived on the coastal islands were easy targets for Cromwell's brutality.

In November 1641, soldiers under the command of Captain Conyngham of Doe Castle sailed to Arranmore Island. The people of the island saw the approaching galleys and hid in a cave along the island's cliffs.

The soldiers plundered the island for seven days while its inhabitants remained hidden. Houses were burned, and valuables were stolen and loaded onto the boats. As the men were preparing to leave the island, they saw a woman near the cave entrance. Soldiers captured her and mercilessly beat and slaughtered the helpless people trapped in the cave. The island's entire population was nearly eliminated. No one knows how many were killed that day, but some sources estimate as many as seventy. The cave is still visited today, but few realize the tragedy that took place in it.

DUNMORE CAVE
Ireland

Dunmore Cave, also called Dearc Fearna (the Cave of the Alders), is a popular tourist attraction and one of several commercial caves in Ireland. The cave has two levels with more than one thousand feet of passage. Early descriptions portray the entrance as "the mouth of a huge beast, with ten thousand teeth over your head and as many under your feet." It is said the demon Luchtigen, Lord of Rats and Mice, was slain in the cave. The cave also contains the tallest stalagmite in Europe.

In 928 AD, Vikings were ransacking many of the coastal villages and settlements of Ireland. Monasteries were favorite targets. They contained a wealth of gold ornaments, and Irish monks seldom put up a fight. As the Vikings moved inland, their rampage had devastating results for the people of the Osraigh tribe.

It is believed that, upon seeing the approaching Vikings, more than one thousand villagers took refuge in Dunmore Cave. What once served as a shelter now became a death trap as the marauding Vikings set fires at the entrance and massacred every person they found. The massacre is documented in the Annals of the Four Masters: "Godfrey, grandson of Imhar, with the foreigners of Ath-cliath, demolished and plundered Dearc Fearna, where one thousand persons were killed . . ." Written by four monks, this work recounts the early history of Gaelic Ireland.

Human bones are frequently found in the cave. In 1973, the bones of forty-four adults and children were discovered in there, and in 1996, explorers found more bones. In late 1999, a worker cleaning up litter in the cave found a cache of Viking artifacts that included coins, bronze and silver ingots, as well as silver ornaments for garments. This find gives added credence to the theory that the cave was a massacre site and has renewed interest in it. The cave is currently closed pending further archeological research and evaluation.

ROCK HOUSE CAVE
New Jersey

On July 4, 1776, John Hart added his signature to the Declaration of Independence. Each man knew that signing this declaration put his life, family, and property at great risk. Months after the signing, British and Hessian troops invaded northern New Jersey and moved swiftly across the state.

British troops reached Princeton in early December and began taking into custody the property and personal belongings of local patriots. Fearing for his life, Hart fled into the heavily wooded Sourland Mountains that surrounded his Hopewell home in Somerset County.

Near Hart's home, the forest floor is strewn with huge boulders and massive piles of rocks that form small talus caves and shelters. The largest is called Rock House Cave. Here John Hart found refuge from his pursuers, and his "life, liberty and the pursuit of happiness" became confined within the walls of a small cave.

Living the life of a fugitive took its toll on the sixty-three-year-old Hart. The damp cave provided little protection from the harsh winter weather. Hart would have surely died had it not been for friends and relatives who secretly brought him food and clothing.

On Christmas night, Washington's men defeated Hessian troops in a surprise attack on Trenton, and on January 3 they won another battle at Princeton. These wins forced British and Hessian occupation out of central New Jersey, allowing John Hart to return to his home and New Jersey government to function again.

John Hart died on May 11, 1779. The Revolutionary War continued for two more years, and Hart never saw his dream of the thirteen colonies free from British threat. Today, the area near the cave is a favorite place for rock climbers. Many pass by the entrance unaware of the role this cave played in our nation's fight for freedom.

MAKKE'DAH CAVE
Judah

Throughout the stories in the Bible, caves are used for shelters, places of worship, as tombs to bury the dead, and as places to hide from one's enemies—sometimes with tragic results. The book of Joshua contains the story of the five kings of the Amorites: Adoni-Zedek, king of Jerusalem; Hoham, king of Hebron; Piram, king of Jarmuth; Japhia, king of Lachish; and Debir, king of Eglon.

After hearing that Joshua and the people of Gibeon had made a treaty of peace with Israel, the five kings of the Amorites combined their armies and attacked the city of Gibeon. The armies of Israel, with a little help from God, successfully protected Gibeon and defeated the armies of all five kings in one battle.

Seeing their armies beaten, the five kings hid in a cave at Makke'dah. They hoped to wait out the battle and then return to their cities; however, the kings were found. Joshua told his men to "roll great stones against the mouth of the cave, and set men by it to guard them; but do not stay there yourselves, pursue your enemies, fall upon their rear, do not let them enter their cities; for the Lord your God has given them into your hand."

After the battle, the stones were removed, and the five kings were captured. Joshua killed the kings and hung their bodies on a tree for all to see. At sunset, he cut them down and threw their bodies back into the cave. The entrance was sealed with large rocks that, according to the Bible story, "remain there to this day."

SUICIDES AND ACCIDENTS

SANDANHEKI CAVERN
Japan

The Pacific Ocean batters a rugged two-mile length of shoreline along the southern coast of Japan. One hundred and fifty-foot cliffs tower above the water's edge, and numerous sea caves dot the jagged shore. The largest is Sandanheki Cavern.

The history of the cave dates back more than one thousand years. Kumano Pirates of the Heian Era used the cave as a secret lair to run their raids on unsuspecting ships. Japanese people have also used the cave as a place of worship. Today, visitors enter the cave via a ninety-foot elevator that descends from the Cavern Visitor Center. Although many come to see the cave and the spectacular vistas the cliffs offer, the area is most noted for its reputation as a suicide destination.

Every year approximately twenty people end their lives by jumping from the cliffs above the cave. Most die on the rocky shore. Some bodies drift out to sea, while others are swept into the cave. Body recovery is a familiar sight in the cave, and tourists may occasionally see a dead body floating in the murky waters. Cavern staff are sometimes required to help talk people out of jumping or to assist the police in locating bodies and moving the departed up the elevator and through the Visitor Center. Signs are posted along the cliff's edge, urging prospective jumpers to think twice before taking the final plunge.

Statistics show that Japan has one of the highest suicide rates of any industrialized country. No one knows for sure why this particular place is so popular for suicides. One theory is that a successful suicide is almost guaranteed from this location. Others believe that the cave is haunted and that the ghosts of the dead are to blame.

CASS CAVE
West Virginia

Clarence Wamsley did not take lightly the report from his doctor. The prognosis was tongue cancer—long before the days of chemotherapy and radiation treatments. He was given two choices: live for three more months with the cancer or remove the tongue and live for possibly one year. For Clarence, there remained a third option. He was a proud man and was not about to let cancer cause him to wither away, nor would he face the uncertainty of surgery and life without his tongue. He would live and die by his own rules.

Early in July 1923, Clarence left his home in Ridgeway, Pennsylvania, and headed to West Virginia. Many years before he had worked in West Virginia at a lumber mill in the town of Cass. It was a place of fond memories and also the location of McLaughlin Cave, known today as Sheets Cave or Cass Cave. Clarence was familiar with the cave, as were many locals who explored its depths. During his journey from Pennsylvania, Clarence stopped in Elkins, West Virginia. There he wrote the following letter to his brother, Floyd, and mailed it with a check for the amount remaining in his savings account.

"I have decided not to have an operation, and will take matters in my own hands and end it all. I know of a place about 100 miles from here where I can get about 50 feet underground. This will be a kind of burial for me. Break the news to mother some way. You look after her and see that her bills are paid for she will forget them. Get her pension check for her. I will never be back in Ridgeway, Pennsylvania. Tell the folks I have gone to Norfolk, Virginia, for my health."

On July 21, Clarence arrived in Cass and wrote his brother another letter stating, "I have about six miles to walk up a mountain. Clarence." Upon receiving the final letter postmarked from Cass, Floyd Wamsley and a friend drove to the town. After talking with locals, they decided that Clarence's final resting place must be McLaughlin Cave.

Floyd entered the cave with a police officer and a United States Deputy Marshall. They found his brother's body one hundred and fifty feet from the entrance. Clarence was sitting against a passage wall with a .42 caliber gun still in his right hand. In front of his right ear, a single bullet had entered his brain and ended his life.

Clarence's body was removed from the cave, followed by a hearing to review all the facts. A jury unanimously decided that Clarence did indeed end his life with a self-inflicted gunshot. Poor Clarence, who thought he would "never be back in Ridgeway," was returned to his family and given a proper burial.

Numerous accidents and deaths continue to haunt

this cave. Small underground streams can quickly turn into raging torrents that trap cavers and expose them to hypothermia. Explorers also face a dangerous one hundred and thirty-nine-foot waterfall drop aptly named Suicide Falls.

MACOCHA ABYSS
Czech Republic

The Macocha Abyss is north of the town of Brno in the heart of the Czech Republic, formerly Czechoslovakia. This pit became exposed when the roof of a huge underground chamber collapsed, forming a chasm almost one thousand feet long, four hundred feet wide, and five hundred feet deep. An underground river feeds two small lakes at the bottom of the pit and continues into the commercialized section of the cave. The history of the pit has been documented back to 1575, but it was not until the early 1700s that it acquired the name Macocha Abyss.

The name comes from a story locals tell about a widower who lived with his son in the nearby village of Vilemovice. After living for several years without a wife, the father remarried. The couple soon had a child of their own, and the vengeful wife wanted no part of her stepson. One morning, the stepmother lured the child to the pit and pushed him over the edge. Fortunately, the young boy became entangled in tree branches growing from the cliff face. A passerby heard his cries for help and managed to pull him to safety. After hearing the news, the husband took justice into his own hands and threw his wife into the black depths of the pit. From that day, the pit was called Macocha: the Czech word for stepmother.

Some of the first descents into the pit were not to explore its depths but to retrieve the bodies of suicide jumpers. The first recorded suicide into the pit occurred in 1829. To date, more than fifty people have ended their lives by jumping into the seemingly bottomless depths of the abyss. Many of the bodies have never been recovered.

NICKAJACK CAVE
Tennessee

In April 1964, the Tennessee Valley Authority (TVA) began construction of Nickajack Dam in southeastern Tennessee. Three and a half years later, the gates of the dam closed, and the waters of the Tennessee River began to rise behind the locks, forming Nickajack Lake. The lake has two hundred and fifteen miles of shoreline and extends forty-six miles upstream.

The dam is named after a cave of the same name found along the lake's edge. Nickajack Cave is one of Tennessee's most famous caves and boasts a massive entrance fifty feet high and one hundred and forty feet wide. Most of the cave has now been submerged, resulting in the loss of a wealth of historical and archeological artifacts.

The large passages and rooms have sheltered Chickamauga Indians as well as notorious river pirates who terrorized travelers along the Tennessee River. During the Civil War, the cave was an important location for the mining of saltpeter—the all-important ingredient for the making of gunpowder. Possession of the cave changed several times during the war, and both Confederate and Union troops took losses defending this site.

After the war, the cave was briefly commercialized; dancing couples and live music filled its large chambers. Prior to its flooding, cave explorers also probed the dark depths of Nickajack Cave and mapped almost one and a half miles of passage. Quite possibly one of the last to walk through the immense chambers of the cave was America's own "Man in Black," Johnny Cash.

By the mid-1960s, Cash was riding the waves of success as country music's most popular performer. His unique sound and style had earned him a string of number one hits and several gold albums. His concerts were selling out around the world, and he was starring in television and movie roles. Yet with all his fame and fortune, Cash was a wounded man. Ten years of drug abuse had taken its toll on his mind and body. He cancelled shows and recording dates, wrecked cars, was on the verge of divorce, and spent time in and out of hospitals and jails. In his book, *Cash: The Autobiography*, he describes himself as "a walking vision of death."

In October 1967, Cash had had enough. His thoughts wandered back to the memories of exploring Nickajack Cave with his good friend Hank Williams, Jr. The dark and isolation of the underground was a befitting place to match his troubled soul and end his life.

Cash parked his Jeep at the cave and walked into the gaping entrance. He walked and crawled for hours until the light from his one flashlight finally faded, leaving him in an alien world of utter darkness. Then he lay down on the cave floor to await a slow hypothermic death. He knew the cave was due to be flooded and his remains would be lost forever in a watery, underground grave.

However, as he lay there, Cash began to feel at peace. His feelings of gloom and despair began to fade. Confused by the sudden change of emotion, he turned his thoughts to God. He believed that God was putting feelings in his heart and telling him it was not his time to die. Yet, how would he ever get out of the hopelessness of the situation he had placed himself in? Feeling an impulse to move, Cash began to crawl. He had no idea which way he should go, but he was determined to leave the cave and change his life for the better.

He inched his way slowly through the darkness, following a soft breeze he knew would lead him out. After crawling for an unknown amount of time, Cash finally saw light streaming in from the outside. At the entrance, he came upon his mother and June Carter holding a basket of food she had brought for him. Together they drove back to Nashville. Cash told them that God had saved him, and he was ready to commit himself to God and to rid his body of drugs. In the following months, he cleaned himself up, married June, recorded another hit album, landed his own television show, and fathered his first son.

Two large fences across the entrance now block entry of boats and people into the cave. Access is also restricted to protect endangered bats that use the cave for hibernation in the winter and for a maternity roost in the summer.

In August 1992, two sport divers illegally entered the cave. They were not trained in cave diving, nor did they possess the proper skills and equipment needed for such a dive. While exploring in the murky water, they became confused about which way was out and separated. One was able to find the entrance, but the other surfaced in a small air chamber deep inside the cave. The companion immediately notified the sheriff and a well-publicized rescue ensued.

To assist in the rescue, the TVA opened the locks of

the dam to lower the water level in the cave, resulting in several hundred thousand dollars of lost electrical generating revenue. Still, seventeen hours passed before divers finally found the lost explorer alive. His air supply was moments away from being exhausted. During his stay in the cave, the man had a vision of angels coming toward him. Many believe that God was once again watching over those who enter Nickajack Cave.

DEVILS DEN
New Jersey

During the American Revolution, bands of American Tories terrorized the thirteen colonies. One of the most famous Tories was James Moody. In early 1777, Moody abandoned his farm in Sussex County, New Jersey, and recruited a secret force of more than five hundred men to fight for the King and wreak havoc across northern New Jersey.

It is rumored that one of his secret hideouts was a cave called Devils Den in Newton, New Jersey. The cave was said to be more than one mile long and adorned with Turkish carpets, chandeliers, mirrors, sofas, and graced with an English grand piano in its center chamber.

One story is that Moody abducted a young woman named Kittatinny, the daughter of a Lenape Indian Chief, and brought her to his wondrous cave. Day and night she was held captive as he tried unsuccessfully to win her love. One night, his maiden was nowhere to be found. Searching the cave, he discovered her lifeless body hanging from a large chandelier. Depressed at being enslaved, she had climbed atop the grand piano and hung herself.

The cave is one of the largest in New Jersey. In 1993, cavers from the Central New Jersey Grotto squeezed through a narrow fissure and discovered an additional three hundred and seventy-five feet of passage. Although the cave shows no sign of its reputed elegance and size, perhaps more passages lie hidden and Moody's treasures are still waiting to be discovered.

SUICIDE CAVE
Indiana

S uicide Cave is ten miles north of Salem, Indiana, and contains more than four thousand feet of passage. The cave earned its name from an unfortunate incident that occurred in the early 1920s. Here is Murl Peugh's (born in 1904) account of what happened that day as told to and recorded by Ed DeJean, a former owner of the cave.

It was a pretty Sunday afternoon late in the summer when three of us young fellers decided that we would go cavin' in the sinkhole cave up over the knobs. We got our coal-oil lanterns all ready, put on our old clothes fer crawlin' through the mud to get into the cave, told our folks where we were goin' and what we were goin' to do, and away we went. I don't remember the exact year, but we were in our late teens or early twenties, so it had to be in the 1920s.

Frank Wingler was lead man, Harry Payne was second, and I was bringing up the rear. We got in in good shape, all our lanterns were up to perfection, and we had moved about 50 or 60 feet beyond the crawl entry to where we were goin' passed a shoulder-high ledge on our left. Frank slid on passed nice and easy, but when Harry put his hand on the ledge fer a better hold, he jerked it back with the same speed with which he sucked in his breath, and then when he could finally turn his wind into words, he stuttered out, "Ther-ther-ther-there's a body up there."

Frank and I knew Harry well enough to know that this was an honest exclamation, so we lifted our lanterns up over the ledge. Sure enough, there was indeed someone in a greasy denim shirt and dark overalls layin' there on his back on that ledge, and he gave every indication of being dead. He was into the cave feet first, so my lantern showed the top of his head, and you could see where blood had run down the back of it from what appeared to be a hole.

I can't say how long our conference was or exactly what we said, but I do remember that we gave absolutely no thoughts to bringin' the body out; but gave every consideration to gettin' ourselves out of there as quick as safety would permit. We came out yellin' fer help and, although we were in a sparsely populated area, we quick drew in all sorts of people.

We said that we'd found a dead man and that we didn't know who it was. Some of those gathered said, "Let's just forget the whole thing and leave him down there." Others just left in a hurry so they wouldn't have to make any decisions. But I remember that Harry Jamison and Roy Ribelin calmed everybody down and said, "Now the thing to do is to get to town as quick as we can and get the sheriff." Jesse Bowling took Ray Williams in his Model-T and they went off to fetch the sheriff.

Frank Wingler, Harry Payne, and I agreed to go part way back into the cave to keep other folks from comin' in and messin' up any evidence. As soon as they yelled that

Sheriff Charlie Moore was there, we came out and got him and showed him how to get back to the body.

The sheriff took a good look and said, "Why, that's Bailey Bowling. We've been lookin' for him since last Thursday." He didn't see fit to confide any more details of the case to us three right then, nor did we see fit to inquire into official business of that nature.

The sheriff said that we couldn't move the body until the coroner had come and made his examination, so this meant another trip to town, finding the coroner, and waiting until he could get there.

Well, when the coroner looked the situation over he ruled that he had no desire to go into the cave. He decreed further that his examination would be conducted in the open air and that the sheriff could just fill him in on any underground information. Everybody agreed that the coroner's portly physique might drag in a few places between where we were and the body, so the sheriff asked for volunteers to bring the body out. Naturally by this time, Frank Wingler, Harry Payne, and I had assumed the role of expert cavers, even if we were inexpert morticians, so we said we'd help. I'm here to tell you that gettin' your own body in and out of a cave is sure a lot easier than gettin' somebody else's out after rigor mortis has set in.

The coroner made a fairly scientific display of examinin' the body. Then he tried to bend the arms and legs and when they wouldn't move much he pronounced his conclusions, "It is impossible to say how long the deceased has been dead due to the fact that his extremities will not flex. It is further apparent that he held a gun to the back of his head and shot himself through the top of the head."

Well, we inexpert morticians knew, from our viewing

the body in the cave with the gun layin' on his chest, that Bailey Bowling had put the gun in his mouth and shot up through. We told the coroner that we doubted that the deceased could have shot himself in the back of the head and then laid the gun down nice and neat on his chest. But do you think that the coroner would listen to us? I'll bet if you go to the courthouse and dig out the report, it will say that, "The deceased shot himself by holding the gun to the back of his head."

One thing was certain; there was never any question that Bailey Bowling had committed suicide. As the sheriff's story came out, it shed a good deal of light on the matter. Bailey Bowling had a little shop about half-way to the County Seat from the cave. He was real good at repairing things like farm machinery, wagons, bicycles, and such. He was also good at workin' metals, it seems. So good in fact that he could bend up all the copper coils and solder up all the connections necessary to make a functional still. There were rumors that he shared some of his distilled product with others for a price. Well, Sheriff Moore and one of his deputies had gone out to Bailey's place on the Thursday before this Sunday to have a chat with him about these sales. The sheriff and his deputy were walking up toward the shop through some real tall weeds when Bailey came to the door of his shop with a gun and suggested that they not come any farther.

The sheriff knew that Bailey was a bit eccentric, some said "odd," but he didn't think he was dangerous, so he just yelled out, "Now, Bailey, we just want to talk." However, conversation never got goin' well at all because Bailey let go first with one barrel and then the other. The two lawmen dropped into the weeds just like they had been shot; maybe even they weren't sure at this point, and stayed there for a sensible period of time.

Bailey Bowling didn't check them out but, fearing the worst, went out the back door of his shop and headed in the direction of the cave. He stopped at a relative's house and told him that he was sure that he had shot the sheriff and a deputy, asked for some food, and told the relative that he would be hidin' out somewhere for awhile. The relative couldn't persuade him to check the matter out, or turn himself in. Nor could he stop his flight.

We always guessed that Bailey just sort of went crazy with conscience and fright, went to the cave, where of course no one could get him word that he hadn't shot anybody, and committed suicide.

One last thing: Ray Williams said several years later that it was a pity that Bailey Bowling went to his reward without gettin' credit fer his contribution to progress. Ray said that Bailey had wanted to saw a dead limb off a real tall tree near his shop for fear it would fall on somebody. He took a bicycle chain and riveted some saw teeth to it, fastened a rope to each end of the bicycle chain, threw one rope over the limb, got the chain centered on the limb, and by pulling the two ropes he sawed the limb off. Ray said Bailey Bowling never got credit fer inventin' the chainsaw.

AMARNATH CAVE
Kashmir

Mount Amarnath, one of the Himalayan Mountains of northern Kashmir, rises fourteen thousand feet above sea level. Just below the summit is Amarnath Cave, one of the holiest sites of the Hindu religion. Its entrance is one hundred and fifty feet high, and the cave extends ninety feet into the mountain.

Amarnath Cave contains a phallus-shaped ice stalagmite that forms from water falling from a natural spring in the back of the cave. This formation is believed to be a representation of the Hindu god Shiva and is said to reach a maximum height of five and a half feet during the full moon. Wild pigeons frequent the cave and are also believed to be symbols of Shiva. Several smaller ice formations form alongside the stalagmite. These represent the Hindu gods Ganesha, Parvati, and Bharirava. A small alcove inside the cave contains a chalk-like substance known as Vibhuti (Holy Ash) that is a sacrament in the worship of Shiva.

Since 1000 BC, worshipers have been making a trek to the cave. According to the legend, in the cave Shiva disclosed the secrets of creation and immortality to his companion Parvati, and those who make the difficult journey to the cave are promised salvation. People from every corner of the world visit the shrine to pay homage to Shiva. Because of the harsh climate and rugged terrain, the cave is accessible only during the monsoon season from July to August.

August 16, 1996, marked the start of the annual pilgrimage. More than one hundred and fifteen thousand people, the most to ever register for the journey, arrived in the towns of Chandanwari and Pahalgam to attempt the treacherous twenty-eight-mile hike to the cave. In former years, attendance had been down because of threats and attacks from Kashmiri militants. This year, instead of rebels, the weather posed the greatest hazard.

Most trekkers try to arrive at the cave during the full moon, which in 1996 was on August 28. Although the area was not known for cold weather at this time of year, on August 22, a severe blizzard roared through the mountains, and the temperature plunged from seventy degrees to below freezing. The storm continued for three days, turning the religious trek into a death march for eighty thousand pilgrims along the route.

Barefoot and poorly equipped for this type of weather, tens of thousands of people struggled from the mountains to the small villages. Thousands were trapped along the upper parts of the trail. Many tried to reach the cave, their only hope of shelter for miles around. The army set up camps wherever possible, but flooded roads and landslides blocked all access for emergency vehicles. Poor visibility and hurricane-force winds also kept air force helicopters from reaching those stranded at high elevations.

The number of deaths rose as pilgrims were swept away by swollen rivers or fell from the crowded, narrow, icy paths into deep ravines hundreds of feet below the trail. Those who were too old or ill to walk and were riding on mules fell to the ground and never got up. After the storm, the mules were used to carry the dead down the mountain. The entire route was littered with bodies. Many of the dead were naked holy men, their bodies covered with ash.

At the cave entrance, twenty inches of snow blanketed the ground. Inside the cave was a macabre scene as the living huddled among the dead for warmth. More than one hundred people died in the cave before rescuers arrived. After the clouds lifted, the army carried down the sick and injured and cremated the dead. In all, two hundred and sixty pilgrims died from exposure, altitude sickness, and heart failure.

This was the second time that storms had killed people during a trek to the cave. In 1969, forty people died in a freak cloudburst high atop the mountain. In August 2000, militants gunned down ninety-seven pilgrims en route to the cave, but still many people continue to risk their lives to visit it.

LIJIA CAVE
Thailand

Lijia Cave is in Khao Laem National Park in the Myanmar border province of Kanchanaburi, Thailand. For years, treasure hunters have explored this limestone cave in search of a fortune left behind by retreating Japanese soldiers at the end of World War II. The hoard is reputed to contain 2,500 tons of gold and 250 United States Federal Reserve gold bullion bonds with a face value of $55 billion.

It is believed the Japanese Imperial Army drove two train cars loaded with the cache into the cave and then dynamited the entrance shut. Local villagers remember train tracks entering the cave; however, no evidence of them is present today. A monk claimed to have entered the cave years ago and to have seen fifty chests full of gold, a steam train, and the skeletons of Japanese soldiers who had committed hara-kiri.

The government of Thailand is also involved in the search and is using satellites and high-tech seismic equipment that can detect large masses of metal. The treasure could easily eliminate Thailand's national debt of $6.2 billion. So far, all results have proved negative. Many suspect that the treasure is the biggest hoax in Thailand's history. Others still believe it will be found and continue to search.

On July 23, 2000, eight treasure hunters illegally entered Lijia Cave. After spending a day digging in the entrance area, the team ventured into the lower levels. As the group descended through the narrow passages, they encountered high levels of carbon dioxide. The first six in the group (four men and two women) did not have the strength to reach the surface and died of asphyxiation in a matter of minutes. Two men were able to exit and called authorities. The following day, the police removed the bodies and promptly sealed the entrance. The two survivors were charged with "forest encroachment" and may face fines and prison sentences for the damage their digging caused.

In April 2001, a sixty-man team made a valiant effort to remove the approximate two thousand tons of dirt and stone believed to be blocking the entrance. Four hundred police and forestry officials were dispatched to control the hundreds of people gathered at the cave, as well as guard any treasure that might be found. Fears of a roof collapse halted the digging. Further excavation is now pending until a safer method is devised.

CAVE OF CRYSTALS
Mexico

One hundred and fifty miles south of the Texas border lies the mining town of Naica, Mexico. Since the late 1700s, a wealth of silver, lead, copper, gold, and zinc have been mined from the surrounding Naica Mountains. These mines also contain the world's largest selenite and gypsum crystals.

The region is known for its abundance of crystals, and sales of them are popular among locals and tourists. The hazards of collecting these crystals are enormous, and many risk their lives doing so. Deep in these mines, temperatures can reach one hundred and fifty degrees with one hundred percent humidity. Many places are unstable, and bad air is always a lurking danger. One miner found out the hard way how quickly treasure can turn into tragedy.

In early April 2000, workers at the Naica Mine discovered a room more spectacular than any previously found. Located more than one thousand feet below the surface, the cathedral-size room contained approximately twenty crystals. Some were fifty feet long and almost six feet in diameter, weighing in excess of ten tons. Work in the tunnel was rerouted to preserve the room. The entrance was sealed with a brick wall and a locked steel door to guard against looters.

Shortly after the discovery of the Cave of the Crystals, a worker managed to find a way into the room through a small hole. He carried a rope, a crowbar, and several plastic bags filled with fresh air. Within minutes of entering the room, he became weak and dizzy. In a panic, he reached for the bags of air, only to find the sharp crystal had punctured them. From the intense heat and lack of air, he collapsed to the floor and died. The following day workers noticed an unusual odor—the smell of roasted flesh and bone. Management has since increased security to the mine.

MURPHYS CAVE
Missouri

The world of caves is no stranger to most people living in Hannibal, Missouri. It is here that Mark Twain's fictional character, Tom Sawyer, lived his life along the banks of the Mississippi River. *The Adventures of Tom Sawyer* has probably encouraged more young children to enter a cave equipped with candles and string than any other book, yet few realize the true dangers of exploring a cave. Missouri has more than 5,600 caves, and finding one is not that hard.

Murphys Cave, also known as Lost Boys Cave, in Hannibal, Missouri, was discovered during shale mining in the 1800s. It has a confusing maze of more than 9,000 feet of passage. In 1873, three young boys entered Murphys Cave and became lost. Rescuers spent several hours searching until the boys were found. After that incident, the entrance was sealed until the 1950s when cavers began exploration.

On May 10, 1967, two brothers and their friend, ages 10, 13, and 14, entered a newly opened entrance to Murphys Cave in Hannibal. Recent highway construction had removed a section of Lovers Leap Hill and exposed the passage. This entrance connected to a then unknown portion of the cave. All three boys were avid readers of Tom Sawyer and loved to explore. They were warned by their parents to stay away from the area, but the lure of playing near a construction site and finding caves was too much to resist. Earlier in the week, they had told a friend about a cave they had found but refused to divulge its location.

Around 5:00 p.m., the boys were seen entering the cave carrying flashlights and a shovel. By 7:00 p.m., they had not returned home, prompting their worried parents to call the police. Immediately, local cavers and members of the Mark Twain Rescue Squad searched the cave but found nothing. Additional cave rescue teams were called in from Missouri, Illinois, Texas, and Washington, DC. The resulting search was one of the largest cave rescue efforts ever undertaken.

Rescue personnel combed the narrow passages of

the cave for days without finding a clue of the boys. In a scene reminiscent from Mark Twain's book, friends, family, and townspeople gathered outside the cave and prayed for the boys' safe return.

Police dogs were also used in the search. In the cave, the dogs' efforts ended at a recent pile of breakdown that sealed off the passage. Workers were unable to dig through the pile, so a new entrance was opened in hopes of bypassing the blockage. Cavers scrambled in but found no sign of the boys.

After thoroughly searching for four days, rescuers began to doubt that the boys were in the cave. With the help of one hundred and fifty National Guardsmen, the search was expanded to other known caves, sinkholes, surrounding woods, and the Mississippi River. Train schedules were checked in the chance the boys had hopped into an open boxcar. Others suspected the boys might have sailed down the river on a rafting adventure.

The story of the lost boys spread across the country. Several psychics called in with their ideas concerning the boys' whereabouts. One had a vision of the boys in a rail-road car loaded with oranges. Another thought the boys would be found twenty-six feet from a piece of heavy equipment, and yet another said the boys were trapped in a drop-off at the end of a passageway in a cave.

On May 14, Mother's Day, the parents of the two missing brothers addressed the country in a nationally televised plea for help. One glimmer of hope came when two children were seen in the Saint Louis area matching the descriptions of the missing boys. They were never seen again.

In a final attempt to locate the boys, road workers dug open a newly laid section of Highway 79. It was feared that the boys had crawled into one of the recently filled sinkholes that had plagued construction in the area, but still no trace of them was found.

After eight frustrating days, the search was officially called off. Hundreds of rescuers returned to their homes, but local cavers, friends, and family continued to search for months. The search efforts cost an estimated $1.5 million, yet all the money in the world could not bring the three boys back home. For the parents, the whereabouts of their sons would forever be in doubt.

On May 10, 1992, twenty-five years to the day after the boys' disappearance, a memorial service was held on Lovers Leap Hill. A bronze marker was unveiled as a permanent reminder of the tragic events. Mayor John Yancey designated May 10 as a Day of Remembrance for the three lost boys. To this day, the boys' disappearance remains a mystery. They simply vanished, never to be seen again.

LEWIS CAVE
New Jersey

Within a cemetery in the town of Newton, New Jersey, is a cave of mysterious nature. Located in a rock wall, it is believed to contain the remains of three young children. A marble plaque seals the entrance. Inscribed on the plaque is the family name "Lewis" and the names of "James W., Margaret M., and J. Howard," dated 1909.

Townspeople say that Margaret loved to play near the rock outcroppings that bordered the cemetery. One day, she wandered into the cave and was never seen again. Two years later, her two brothers died of pneumonia and were buried in the same place that Margaret disappeared.

Rumors have circulated for years of a large cave system under Newton. Although cavers have yet to find a way into it, perhaps Margaret Lewis did.

WEIRDNESS AND THE UNEXPLAINED

BELL WITCH CAVE
Tennessee

The legend of the Bell Witch is one of the oldest and most documented ghost stories in the USA. It is the tale of a ghost gone wild.

In 1817, shortly after John Bell and his family arrived at their new farm near Adams, Tennessee, strange things began to occur. Knocking, banging, and scratching were heard in their house. Glassware and plates suddenly flew across the room as if tossed by unseen hands. At night while the Bells slept, blankets were pulled off their bodies and their pillows were thrown to the floor.

Soon an apparition appeared and began to communicate with the Bell family. The female spirit identified herself as a witch. The Bells were told that it was the tormented soul of Kate Batts, a local woman with whom many did not get along. The spirit, however, also claimed to be the ghost of a young girl from North Carolina, and on another occasion professed to be the ghost of someone buried on the Bells' property.

As the months passed, the harassment and physical abuse became more severe. Kate enjoyed tormenting twelve-year-old Betsy Bell the most. Betsy claimed that the ghost kicked and scratched her, stuck her with pins, pulled her hair, and slapped her face. Word spread of the Bell Witch, and many stopped by the Bells' house to experience the strange goings on. Few left disappointed. General Andrew Jackson visited their home and witnessed Kate's antics stating, "I would rather fight the entire British army than deal with the Bell Witch." Kate also made appearances throughout the county. She enjoyed drinking corn whiskey and making a ruckus. After claiming responsibility for the poisoning death of John Bell, Kate disappeared from the house, and it is said that she then took up residency in a cave on the Bells' farm.

The cave, located in a bluff along the south side of the Red River, contains about seven hundred and fifty feet of passage on two levels. A stream runs out of the entrance to form a forty-foot waterfall that cascades down to the river.

Numerous stories persist about unusual happenings in the cave. Paranormal researchers claim to have discovered high energy levels in the cave. Visitors have reported strange sounds, eerie feelings, and sightings of apparitions. In the cave, camera equipment has jammed and film has rewound for no apparent reason. Photographs taken in the cave sometimes reveal floating white or orange orbs of a type said to be common in locations associated with paranormal activity. A few people have even reported seeing a dark-haired woman drifting throughout the cave.

The land above the cave was a burial ground for Choctaw Indians. In the cave is an empty Indian grave. The skeleton was stolen in the late 1970s and has never been returned. Some believe that Indian spirits, not the Bell Witch, haunt the cave.

The Bell Witch Cave is open to the public from May 1 to October 31. The current (2004) owners, Chris and Walter Kirby, have owned the property for ten years and have experienced their own share of bizarre happenings. A trip into the cave is not for the meek. Chris Kirby refuses to go into the cave alone. Although the Kirbys have not seen any ghosts, they have heard unusual sounds such as low growling, rocks banging, and the sound of someone running through the water. Many tours have been cut short because a fearful guest insisted on returning to the surface. In their house, the Kirbys have heard doors rattling and footsteps across the floor.

One of the scariest stories they tell is about the time their usually calm eighty-pound Labrador Retriever suddenly grew tense and began growling and barking in the cave. With teeth showing and his hair standing up, he stared at a rock wall, poised to attack. He eventually calmed down but stayed close to his owner until they left the cave.

To this day, no logical explanations have been found for the weird happenings on the property. Maybe it is just our imaginations running wild, but then again, maybe there are some questions better left unanswered.

MARK TWAIN CAVE
Missouri

Mark Twain Cave in Hannibal, Missouri, is the state's first and most celebrated commercial cave. Much of Mark Twain's 1876 book, *The Adventures of Tom Sawyer*, centers on McDougals Cave (properly called McDowells Cave, or known today as Mark Twain Cave) and the adventures that Tom and his friends had there. The cave also has a bizarre tale of which few are aware.

In 1819, Jack Simms first discovered the cave when he followed the tracks of a panther to a small opening in a hill. Explorers described the cave as a "tangled wilderness of narrow and lofty clefts and passages" totaling more than two miles in length. Mark Twain wrote in his autobiography: "No man knew the cave; that was an impossible thing." Word of the cave spread across the Mississippi Valley, and it became a popular stop for people traveling in riverboats along the Mississippi River.

In 1849, Dr. Joseph Nash McDowell purchased the cave and sealed the entrance with a heavy wooden door. McDowell was a well-known and eccentric surgeon from Saint Louis, Missouri. His abrupt closure of the cave was the talk of the town. For young mischievous children, finding another way in was only a matter of time.

After hearing descriptions of what their children had found in the cave, townspeople broke down the wooden door and discovered the truth to their children's wild tales. Hanging from the cave ceiling, suspended by cables, was a glass cylinder enclosed in a copper cylinder. The top was open to allow viewing of the alcohol-embalmed body of McDowell's fourteen-year-old daughter who had died from a childhood disease. Twain wrote of the macabre scene: "Loafers and rowdies used to drag it up by the hair and look at the dead face."

McDowell confessed he was using the cave to experiment with methods of preservation. Many believed McDowell's efforts were genuine. He was aware that two-thousand-year-old mummies found in Mammoth Cave stayed well-preserved. His daughter remained in the cave for two more years until, under pressure from locals, she was removed and placed in a private vault.

McDowell died in 1868. Although his wish of being mummified and buried in Mammoth Cave was never carried out, it certainly would have been a befitting end to a bizarre tale.

CAVE OF THE WITCHES
Spain

In the Pyrenees Mountains of northern Spain, near the border of France, lies the small town of Zugarramurdi. This is Basque Country, encompassing seven provinces, and extending into southwest France. The Basque people are one of the oldest surviving ethnic groups in Europe, and for centuries they have been persecuted in their struggle for independence and political autonomy.

During the 1500s and 1600s, fears of witches and sorcerers swept across Europe. Areas of northern Spain were thought to be breeding grounds for witchcraft. The Basques bore the brunt of witch-hunts by inquisitors wanting to purify the countryside. Those believed to be witches were sentenced to torture, flogging, imprisonment, and execution.

Basque customs strongly influenced Spanish ideas concerning witches. Many of the Basque gods, goddesses, and deities lived underground. The caves near Zugarramurdi were sacred places and were said to be the home of the Basque goddess Mari, the supreme goddess of the underworld and queen to all witches. At times, Mari assumed the identity of a black billy goat known as Akerbeltz. Villagers would gather in the caves to hold an akelarre (a witches sabbath) in her honor with wild dances, sacrifices, and orgies. Christians looked upon Mari as the Devil, and any women who took part in these acts were assumed to be witches.

In 1610, the Spanish Inquisition rounded up forty women from Zugarramurdi who were thought to be practicing witchcraft in a cave. In all likelihood, these women were simply involved in a celebration of the sun. Twelve of the women were accused of being possessed by the Devil and were burned alive in front of a crowd of 30,000 onlookers. From that day, the cave was called the Cave of the Witches, and every year since then, people have gathered in honor of the murdered women.

Today, the tradition continues at the cave with a ceremony held every year during the summer solstice. People dress as witches and wizards; they perform wild dances and offer drinks of magic potions. For most, it is a time of fun and games, but a select few take this ceremony quite seriously.

NTAVELIS CAVE
Greece

Greece contains more than seven thousand caves, many of them noted for their rich historic, archeological, and mythological significance. The stories in Greek mythology are filled with trips into the underworld. The ancient Greeks believed that caves were doorways to a vast kingdom of the dead, ruled by the god Hades.

Zeus, the king of all gods, was born in a cave, as was Hermes, the god of travelers. Artemis (the goddess of fertility) and Somnus (the god of sleep) resided in a cave. Aeolos, the god of wind and air, kept his winds locked in a cave. Harpies—filthy, winged monsters, with the faces of women and the bodies of vultures—lived in caves. Cacus, a fire-breathing troll, was a cave dweller. Polyphemus, a Cyclops, lived underground and survived on meals of human flesh, and Typhon, the scourge of mankind, lived in a cave. Thus, it comes as no surprise that modern Greeks have a few beliefs of their own about the caves in Greece.

Ntavelis Cave, located in a marble quarry on Mount Penteli near the city of Athens, is named after a famous Greek outlaw who used the site as a hideout during the nineteenth century. Marble was mined from this quarry to make the Parthenon and the Acropolis. The entrance to the cave contains a small Byzantine church. Deeper in the cave is an ancient temple dedicated to the Greek god Pan. Several passages go for great distances, and the full extent of the cave unknown.

Over the years, Mount Penteli and particularly Ntavelis Cave have gained notoriety with UFO enthusiasts. Hundreds of people have reported strange lights coming from the area of the cave, along with unusual noises, paranormal activity, and sightings of alien-looking beings. Paranormal researchers working in the cave have observed unexplainable abnormalities in magnetic fields and difficulties in using photographic equipment. It is also noteworthy that an alarming number of people have disappeared after visiting the cave. One researcher believes that the cave is a type of portal or entrance to another dimension. Others claim it is home to an underground civilization of unknown beings.

Years ago, the Greek air force closed the area and began building a large tunnel system in the cave, stating that it was a NATO project. Many workers reported glowing objects and strange sounds during the construction. After years of work, the project was suddenly stopped and the air force abandoned the area. Today, groups of people meet in the cave to meditate and to absorb the energy the cave is said to hold.

Is the cave a dimensional portal to another time and place, or home to a colony of aliens or underground beings? Could there be some truth to the stories the Greeks wrote about their journeys to the underworld?

KITUM CAVE
Africa

In east Africa along the Kenya-Uganda border, Mount Elgon rises out of the rain forest to a height of 14,178 feet. This extinct volcano is the eighth highest mountain on the African continent. Eight thousand feet up its eastern slope lies Kitum Cave, the largest of several caves in Mount Elgon National Park. The cave is a popular tourist stop for trekkers. Many come to see the picturesque waterfall that cascades down its huge entrance. Others hope to catch a glimpse of the herds of elephants that enter the cave at night and gouge the walls with their tusks to dislodge and eat the much-needed salt deposits found in the rocks.

It is believed that elephants carved the immense chambers of this six-hundred-foot-long cave. Seventy of the huge animals can fit into the cave at one time. Many animals, including rats, bats, monkeys, baboons, leopards, buffalos, and millions of insects, frequent the cave. In the dark, predator and prey eat side by side, unaware of each other's presence. Even for the animals, the cave can be a dangerous place. Elephants have been killed by rockfalls caused by their overeager mining. Poachers are also aware of the cave and the attraction the animals have for it.

The walls and ceiling of the cave are made of solidified ash and mud and sparkle with pure white salt crystals. Petrified logs and white bones protrude from the hard rock. These are relics from a past eruption of Mount Elgon. The floor consists of a spongy mix of animal dung that ranges from wet and slimy to bone dry.

Yet it is not the crystals or the elephants nor its enormous size for which Kitum Cave is most noted. Scientists believe that Marburg virus, a strain of the Ebola virus, once lived and perhaps still does live in the dark recesses of the cave.

On January 1, 1980, Charles Monet explored Kitum Cave for several hours. Seven days later, he developed severe headaches and eye pain. Within ten days, he became nauseated, and his skin turned yellow and spotted with brilliant red speckles.

Local doctors had never seen anything like this and quickly put Monet on a plane to the Nairobi Hospital. At the hospital, his symptoms worsened and his skin turned black and blue. His muscle tissue and organs were liquefying, while he continually vomited a black liquid of blood and intestinal lining. In his final hours, his body erupted with blood from every opening. As if by magic, the virus disappeared for seven years.

In August 1987, while vacationing with his parents, ten-year-old Peter Cardinal was admitted to the Nairobi Hospital with pneumonia-like symptoms. Within days, he turned black and blue and his skin filled with pockets of blood. He was diagnosed with Marburg virus and died several days later. Besides having died of Marburg virus, Peter Cardinal and Charles Monet had one more thing in common. Each had been in Kitum Cave a week before their illness. Coincidence?

In spring 1988, the Kenyan government agreed to a

joint Kenya-US expedition to search the cave for a host of the virus. Teams of scientists stayed at the cave and tested thousands of blood and tissue samples from birds, animals, and insects. Caged animals were placed in the cave to see if they acquired the disease, but no trace of the virus was found. It had simply vanished again.

To this day, a host has never been discovered. Hundreds of people have died from this extremely contagious and lethal virus that appears and disappears seemingly at random. Of the few clues found by scientists, Kitum Cave is the only link between two outbreaks. Surely, the virus is still multiplying in an unsuspecting host. Where and when it will reappear again, one can only guess.

CAVE OF TREASURES
Eden

"And the Lord God planted a garden in Eden, in the east; and there he put the man whom he had formed." As we all know, it was not always paradise in the Garden of Eden. The life of Adam and Eve are documented in several books written by Egyptians. These books contain stories dating back to a few hundred years before the birth of Christ.

In *The First Book of Adam and Eve*, after they ate from the Tree of Knowledge, God cast them out of the Garden and sent them to its western border—a strange broad land, covered in sand, strewn with stones, and void of all vegetation. There God commanded them to live in the Cave of Treasures, away from the sweet smells of flowers and fruit, and far from the seas where they could be cleansed of all their sins. Although they were not allowed to return to the Garden, they were given three treasures from it to keep in the cave: gold, incense, and myrrh.

In the beauty of the Garden, Adam and Eve had never seen darkness. In the cave, they were terrified of it. One day, the cave filled with a bright light. Adam and Eve sang praise, thinking their prayers were answered. Their joy was short-lived, as an angel appeared and told them that Satan, the hater of all good, had taken the form of light to trick them into worshiping him. The angel showed them the truth by transforming Satan back into his hideous form. Another day, Satan beat Adam and Eve in the cave and left them for dead. On another occasion, Satan built a fire at the cave's entrance. The heat burned off their clothes and scorched their bodies. Another time, he tried to kill Adam and Eve by rolling a large rock down a hill and into the cave. On the eighty-ninth day of their stay, Satan tried to persuade them to come out by transforming himself into a meek old man who promised them a comfortable place of rest. Fourteen times in all, Satan appeared to Adam and Eve. Although he was persistent, his plans always seemed to go awry and did nothing more then terrorize Adam and Eve.

In *The Second Book of Adam and Eve*, the first couple are married with two sons named Cain and Abel. As the boys grew older, Cain became jealous of Abel and devised a wicked plan to lure his brother to a lonely field. Once there, Cain picked up a large rock and "beat his brother's head with it, until his brains oozed out, and he wallowed in his blood, before him." When Adam and Eve heard of the murder, they found Abel and brought him to the Cave of Treasures. They wrapped Abel in sweet spices and myrrh and buried him in the cave. When Adam died at the age of 930, he, too, was laid to rest in the cave.

The Cave of Treasures is mentioned more than two

hundred and forty times in the books of Adam and Eve.

The cave became a family shrine, and many generations would come to live, die, and be buried there. Many believe that the Garden of Eden was in Egypt and that the cave and its treasures may still be waiting to be discovered. As for the Devil, well, he might still be there, too.

Acknowledgments

I would like to thank the following people and organizations for their help and support of this book.

Karel Absolon, Oz Backman, Hal Baker, Rosemary Balister, Jerry Baum, Gary Berdeaux, Jill Biel, Mark Botkin, Roger Brucker, Dave Bunnell, Cave Research Foundation, Don Coons, Dave and Sandra Cowan, George Dasher, Emily Davis, Joe Douglas, Kevin Downey, Don Dunham, Marshall Fausold, Richard Fisher, Amos Frumkin, Edward Greene, Chuck Hemple, Bob Hoff, Michael Hollahan, Chris Howes, Leela Hutchison, Ronal Kerbo, Ray Keeler, Chris and Walter Kirby, Larry Matthews, Roger McClure, Marian McConnell, Andrej Mihevc, Bill Mixon, Wm. Michael Mott, Gerald Moni, Bobbi Nagy, National Park Service, National Speleological Society, Bob Nordgren, Tony Oldham, Colleen Olson, Tom Pollock, Chuck Porter, Tom Rea, Red Oak Nature Center, Bruce Rogers, Jo Schaper, Roberta Serface, Marion Smith, Greg Springer, Michael Taylor, Troy Taylor, Bill Torode, John Tudek, Richard Turner, Eva Tsourounakis, Chris Watson, Red Watson, James Webster, West Virginia State Police, Keith Wheeland, Elizabeth Winkler, Mark Wolinsky, Mike Zawada.

If you are interested in pursuing cave exploration after reading this book, I suggest you first contact the National Speleological Society at: <www.caves.org>. They can direct you to organized caving groups in your area.

Bibliography

Amarnath Cave
"Amarnath: Temples of the Himalayas." TempleNet Website.
<http://www.templenet.com/himalaya.html> (10/24/2003).
"Deadly Weather Hits Hindu Pilgrimage, 160 Perish." *Catholic World News*, Aug. 27, 1996. <www.cwnews.com/news/views tory.cfm?recnum=1669> (10/24/2003).
Mirza, Qaiser. "Holy Pilgrimage Turns to Death March." *The News-Times*, Aug. 27, 1996. <www.newstime.com/>.
Mushtaq, Sheikh. "Dead Hindus From Cold Heat Wave." *BurmaNews*, Aug. 24, 1996. <www.euroburma.com/>.
Noatay, K. L. "An Arduous, Yet Exhilarating Experience." *The Tribune*, July 8, 2000. <http://www.tribuneindia.com/2000/20000708/windows/main4.htm> (10/24/2003).
Spaeth, Anthony. "Hindus Trekking Into the Himalayas to Worship Shiva Suffer Terrible Losses to Forces of Nature." *Time*, Sep. 9, 1996. <www.time.com/>.
Apache Death Cave
Backman, Alan (Oz). Personal communication, 2002.
Harrison, Greg. "Highway of Dreams: Part 2." HHJM Website. Reprinted from the *American Motorcyclist* magazine.

<www.hhjm.com/66/static/highway2.htm> (10/24/2003).

"Two Guns." Ghost Towns Website. <www.ghosttowns.com/states/az/twoguns.html> (10/24/2003).

Ardeatine Caves

Duncan, George. "Massacres and Atrocities of WWII." George Duncan's Historical Facts of the Second World War Website. <www.members.iinet.net.au/~gduncan/massacres.html#italy> (10/24/2003).

Katz, Robert. *Death in Rome*. New York: The Macmillan Company, 1967.

Trevelyan, Raleigh. *Rome 44: The Battle for the Eternal City*. New York: Viking, 1981.

Bat Cave

"Five Killed for Bat Dung in Thailand." *BBC News*, Apr. 5, 1998. <http://news.bbc.co.uk/1/hi/world/asia-pacific/74168.stm> (10/24/2003).

Bell Witch Cave

Barr, Tom. *Caves of Tennessee*. Tennessee: Department of Conservation and Commerce, 1961.

Blackman, W. Halden. *The Field Guide to North American Hauntings*. New York: Three Rivers Press, 1998.

Bolte, Mary. *Dark and Bloodied Ground*. New York: Hawthorn Books, Inc., 1973.

Fitzhugh, Patrick A. The Bell Witch Website. <www.bellwitch.org/home.htm> (10/24/2003).

Kirby, Chris. Personal communication, 2001.

Taylor, Troy. "Haunted Tennessee: The Bell Witch." Ghosts of the Prairie Website. <http://www.prairieghosts.com/b-cave.html> (10/24/2003).

Betty Moody Cave

Chan, Terry. The AFU & Urban Legend Archive Website, May 11, 1993. <http://www.urbanlegends.com/death/baby.smothering/smothering_crying_baby.html> (10/24/2003).

"Isle of Shoals History." Isles of Shoals Website. <www.islesofshoals.com/>.

"Welcome to Star Island." Star Island Website. <www.starisland.org/starinfo.html> (10/24/2003).

Blackman Cave

"Blackman Suspect Pleads Not Guilty to Rape." *CNN*, Feb. 27, 2001. <www.cnn.com/2001/WORLD/asiapcf/east/02/27/japan.trial.obara/> (10/24/2003).

"Family Bring Butchered Girl's Remains Home." *CNN*, Mar. 3, 2001. <www.cnn.com/2001/WORLD/asiapcf/east/03/03/japan.blackman/index.html> (10/24/2003).

"Japan Police Charge Hostess Murder Suspect." *CNN*, Apr. 6, 2001. <www.cnn.com/2001/WORLD/asiapcf/east/04/06/japan.rapist/> (10/24/2003).

"New Clue Found in Briton Murder Hunt." *CNN*, Feb. 17, 2001. <http://www.cnn.com/2001/WORLD/europe/UK/02/17/japan.briton/> (10/24/2003).

Wright, Evan A. "Death of a Hostess." *Time*, May 14, 2001. <www.time.com/time/asia/news/magazine/0,9754,108848,00.html> (10/24/2003).

Carlsbad Caverns

Barton, Gene. "Liquor Not Factor in Cavenapping." *The Albuquerque Tribune*, Aug. 6, 1979.

Cantwell, Ned. "Terror Touches Publisher, Hostages." *Current-Argus*, July 11, 1979.

Cantwell, Ned. "Carlsbad Publisher Tells of Hours in Subterranean Ordeal." *Albuquerque Journal*, July 12, 1979.

Lopez, Edward A. "Carlsbad Caverns Incident Report No. 079178." July 10, 1979. U. S. Department of the Interior.

O'Hearn, Jim. "Four Get Misdemeanor Charges." *Current-Argus*, July 30, 1979.

Cass Cave

Botkin, Mark. "Suicide in McLaughlin Cave." *The West Virginia Caver*, June 1999.

Clarkson, Roy B. *On Beyond Leatherbark: The Cass Saga*. West Virginia: McClain Printing, 1990.

Ingalls, Huntley. "The Exploration of Cass Cave, W. Va." *Bulletin of the National Speleological Society*, Jan. 1959.

Castle Royal Caves

Jensen, Duane. "Drunks, Cops, Petty Criminals, and Backgammon Players." Twin Cities Backgammon Club Website. <www.twincitiesbackgammon.org/inlate1970s.html> (10/24/2003).

"Wabasha Street Caves." *The Minnesota Daily*. <www.mndaily. com/>.

Wabashas Street Caves Website. <www.wabashastreetcaves.com/> (10/24/2003).

Catawba Murder Hole

"The Legend of Catawba Murder Hole." The Virginia Region

Website. Reprinted from the *VPI Grotto Grapevine*, Mar. 3, 1944. <www.varegion.org/var/theVar/history71/ pg189Ctawaba.html> (10/24/2003).

McConnell, Marian. Personal communication, 2001.

Cave Home

"69 Killed, 85 Injured in Dynamite Explosion in Shaanxi Province." *People's Daily Online*, July 20, 2001. <www.fpeng.peopledaily.com.cn/200107/20/eng20010720_ 75460.html> (10/24/2003).

"Cave-blast Suspect Surrenders to Police." *CRI Online*, July 17, 2001. <www.web12.cri.com.cn/english/2001/Jul/23366. htm> (10/24/2003).

"Man Over Deadly Cave Village Blast Charged." *People's Daily Online*, Aug. 29, 2001. <www.fpeng.peopledaily.com.cn/ 200108/29/eng20010829_78764.html> (10/24/2003).

"Toll in China Blast up to 69." *CNN*, July 19, 2001. <www.cnn.com/2001/WORLD/asiapcf/east/07/19china. blast.69/?related> (10/24/2003).

Cave of Crystals

Fisher, Richard. Personal communication, 2002.

Hutchinson, Leela. "Leela's Story." <www.naaz.com/>.

Lazcano, Carlos. "Naica's Subterranean Marvels." Translation by Margot Shackelford. *NSS News*, June 2001.

Taylor, Michael Ray. "Huge Natural Crystals Found In Cave." *Discovery News*, Feb. 8, 2001. <www.discovery.com/>.

Cave of Death

Contreras, Franc. "More Than 30 Skulls Found in Cave." *La Prensa San Diego*, May 15, 1998. <www.laprensa-sandiego .org/archieve/may15/skulls.htm> (10/24/2003).

"Mexican Cave of Death!" Tabloid Website, May 13, 1998. <www.tabloid.net/1998/05/13/E1.html> (10/24/2003).

Cave of Letters

Freund, Richard A., and Rami Arav. "Return to the Cave of Letters: What Still Lies Buried?" *Biblical Archaeology Review*, Jan./Feb. 2001.

Webster, James, and Philip Reeder. "Caver Participation in Historic Cave of letters Expedition." *NSS News*, Jan. 2001.

Yadin, Yigael. *Bar-Kokhba: The Rediscovery of the Legendary Hero of the Last Jewish Revolt Against Imperial Rome.* Great Britain: Weidenfeld and Nicolson, 1971.

Cave of the Crying Stream

Catalinotto, John. "Pentagon Gave Orders for War Crimes." *Workers World News Service*, Jan. 13, 2000.<www.lists.peace link.it/yugoslavia/msg00049.html> (10/24/2003).

Choe, Sang-Hun. "Witnesses Say U.S. Bombs Set Off Cave Inferno, Killed Hundreds." Pulitzer Prizes Website. <www.p ulitzer.org/year/2000/investigative-reporting/works/AP11. html> (10/24/2003).

Choe, Sang-Hun, Charles J. Hanley, and Martha Mendoza. "Korean, U.S. Witnesses, Backed by Military, Say Refugees Were Strafed." Pulitzer Prizes Website. <www.pulitzer.org/ year/2000/investigative-reporting/works/AP10.html> (10/29/2003).

Cave of the Patriarchs

"The Cave of Machpelah, Tomb of the Patriarchs." Jewish Virtual Library Website. <www.us-israel.org/jsource/Judaism /machpelah.html> (10/29/2003).

Gross, Avram. "Dr. Baruch Goldstein." The Jewish Community Website, Feb. 26, 1994. <www.herbron.com/>.

"Palestinian Eyewitnesses Tell About The massacre." The Jewish Community Website. <www.herbron.com/>.

Cave of the Slaughter

"The Cave of the Slaughter." How's the Craic? Website. <www.howsthecraic.com/> (10/29/2003).

Cave of the Witches

"Basque Mythology and Pantheon." <www.onetel.net/>.

"The Caves of Zugarramurdi." Hoteles Pamplona Website. <www.hotelespamplona.com/ingles2/rutas/piriat.html> (10/29/2003).

Dashu, Max. Excerpts from *Secret History of the Witches*. Suppressed Histories Website. <www.suppressedhistories.net /secret_history/xorguinas.html> (10/29/2003).

"Spain." Global Harvest Ministries Website.<www.globalharve st.org/index.asp?action=spain> (10/29/2003).

Cave of Treasures

The First Book of Adam and Eve. Hidden Mysteries Website. <www.hiddenmysteries.com/freebook/adameve/adamevetoc. htm> (10/29/2003).

Platt, Rutherford H., and J. Alden Brett. *The Forgotten Books of Eden: Lost books of the Old Testament*. New York: Random House, 1960.

The Second Book of Adam and Eve. Hidden Mysteries

Website. <www.hiddenmysteries.com/freebook/adameve2/
adameve2-toc.html> (10/29/2003).

Dead Man Cave

Franz, Richard, and Dennis Slifer. *The Caves of Maryland.*
Educational Series No. 3. Maryland: Maryland Geological
Survey, 1971.

Dead Mans Hole

"Dead Man's Hole." Bill Strain's Creative Imaging Website.
<www.billstrain.net/hole.html> (10/29/2003).

"Dead Man's Hole." The Handbook of Texas Online Website.
<www.tsha.utexas.edu/handbook/online/articles/view/DD/
rpd3.html> (10/29/2003).

McLeod, Gerald E. "Day Trips." *The Austin Chronicle,* June
11–17, 1999. <www.austinchronicle.com/issues/vol18/issue
41/cols.daytrips.html> (10/29/2003).

Devils Cave

"The legend of Devil's Cave." Red Oak Nature Center
Handout, Illinois.

O'Donnell, Mabel. *Singing Wheels.* New York: Row, Peterson
and Company, 1940.

Devils Den

Adalman, Gary, and Timothy Smith. *Devil's Den: A History
and Guide.* Pennsylvania: Thomas Publications, 1997.

Devils Den

Dalton, Richard F. *The Caves of New Jersey.* Ross Eckler,
"History and Legends of N. J. Caves." New Jersey: New
Jersey Geological Survey, 1976.

Devils Hole

Berketa, Rick. "Devil's Hole and the Devil's Hole Massacre."
Thunder Alley Website. <www.iaw.com/~fallsdevilhole.
html> (10/30/2003).

Berton, Pierre. *Niagara: A History of the Falls.* New York:
Penguin Books, 1992.

Blackman, W. Halden. *The Field Guide to North American
Hauntings.* New York: Three Rivers Press, 1998.

Ensminger, Scott A. *The Caves of Niagara County New York.*
New York: The Niagara County Historical Society, 1987.

Dungeon Cave

Absolon, Karel B. *The Conquest of the Caves and Underground
Rivers of Czechoslovakia's Macocha Abyss: A Historical and
Technical Study of Their Exploration.* Maryland: Kabel

Publishers, 1987.
Dunmore Cave
  Buckley, Laureen. "Dunmore Cave: A Viking Massacre Site."
    <www.xs4all.nl/~tbreen/PAISN/3-DUNMORE.html>
    (10/30/2003).
  "Caves of Ireland: Dunmore Caves." Show Caves Website.
    <www.showcaves.com/english/ie/index.html> (10/30/2003).
  "Viking Items in Ireland Mystifying." *The Japan Times*, Jan. 16,
    2000. <www.trussel.com/prehist/news176.htm> (11/1/2003).
Escape Cave
  "A Brief History of Alcatraz." Federal Bureau of Prisons
    Website. <www.bop.gov/ipapg/ipaalcatraz.html>
    (11/1/2003).
  "Alcatraz Island." National Park ServiceWebsite.<www.nps.gov
    /alcatraz/tours/circ-nav/stop4.html> (10/30/2003).
  Delgado, James P. *Alcatraz: The Story Behind the Scenery.*
    Nevada: KC Publications, 1985.
  "Escape Fails After Four Leap Into Bay"; "Two Shot And
    Drown, Two Captured"; "Former Public Enemy No. 1 and
    Bank Robber Killed"; "Karpis Mobster Found Hiding in
    Cave"; "Four Freedom-hungry Desperadoes Cracked Out
    of Alcatraz in a Thick Fog Early Yesterday"; "Tough Careers
    Lie Behind 'The Rock' Break." *San Francisco Chronicle*,
    Apr. 14, 1943. Zpub Website. <www.zpub.com/sf50/alcatraz/
    sfoealc8.htm> (10/30/2003).
  "Hunter Faces 15 Years More, Loses Parole." *San Francisco
    Chronicle*, Apr. 15, 1943. Zpub Website. <www.zpub.com/
    sf50/alcatraz/sfoealc8.htm> (10/30/2003).
  "Last Convict of Escape Quartet Found on Island." *San
    Francisco Chronicle*, Apr. 17, 1943. Zpub Website. <www.z
    pub.com/sf50/alcatraz/sfoealc8.htm> (10/30/2003).
Feles Cave
  "Feles Cave; Roymata, Ancient King of Vanuatu; Colonial
    History of Vanuatu; The Geography of Vanuata." Vanuatu
    Tourism Website. <www.vanuatutourism.com/> (11/1/2003).
Foster Cave
  Hennop, Jan. "A Night in the Shadow of History." *Sunday
    Times*, Sep. 19, 1999. <http://www.suntimes.co.za/1999/09/
    19/arts/gauteng/aneg05.htm> (10/31/2003).
  Hennop, Jan. "Crimes of the Century." *Sunday Times*, Dec.
    12, 1999. <www.suntimes.co.za/1999/12/12/insight/in02.

htm> (10/31/2003).

Marsh, Rob. "Public Enemy Number One: The Foster Gang: 1914." <www.africacrime-mystery.co.za/books/fsacchp2. htm> (10/31/2003).

Ghost Cave
"Chinese Anti-Rajah Movement 1857." The Bau Town Website. <www.bau.com.my/History1d.htm> (10/31/2003).

Remek, Paul. "A Brief History of Bau." <www.ace.cdc.abu.com/ ~paular/history.html> (10/31/2003).

Ritchie, James. "Ghost Cave of the 1857 Bau Massacre, Sarawak." Aug. 9, 2001. E-Borneo Website. <www.e-borneo .com/cgi-bin/np/viewnews.cgi?category=3&id=997325035> (10/31/2003).

Hariton Cave
"Israel on Trail of Tekoa Teen Murderers." *Worthy News*, May 11, 2001. <www.worthynews.com/news-features/inside-mid-east-peace-372.html> (10/31/2003).

Kiley, Sam. "Two Israeli Boys Stoned to Death in Desert Cave." *The Times*, May 10, 2001. <www.thetimes.co.uk/>.

Laub, Karin. "Two Israeli Boys Stoned to Death Sharon Says Arafat No Longer Partner." *CNews*, May 9, 2001. <www.canoe.ca/>.

McAllester, Matthew. "West Bank Community Suffers Loss of Two Sons." *The Age*, May 11, 2001. <www.theage.com/>.

"Tow Israeli Youths Murdered Near Tekoa." *The Jerusalem Post*, May 9, 2001. <www.jpost.com/>.

Kingsley Cave
"Cultural History of Lassen Park." Shastahome Website. <www.shastahome.com/lassen-volcanic/content.htm> (10/31/2003).

Heizer, R. F., and M. A.Whipple. *California Indians: A Source Book*. California: University of California Press, 1973.

Kroeber, Theodora. *Ishi in Two Worlds: A Biography of the Last Wild Indian in North America*. California: University of California Press, 1976.

May, James. "Spirit of Ishi Finally Free to Join Ancestors." *Indian Country Today*, Aug. 23, 2000. <www.indiancountry. com/?695> (10/31/2003).

Kitum Cave
"Mount Elgon National Reserve." Kilimanjaro Adventure Travel Website. <www.kilimanjaro.com/kenya/mtelgon.htm>

Bibliography

(1/5/2004).

Preston, Richard. *The Hot Zone*. New York: Random House, 1994.

Kocevski Rog

Collis, Brad. "Slovenia's Dark Secret." Ursula's History Website, Apr. 24, 1997. <www.members.tripod.com/~Nevermore/slovene.html> (10/31/2003).

McAdams, C. Michael. "Yalta and the Bleiburg Tragedy." Chapter from the book *Od Bleiburga do Nasih Dana*. <www.ess.uwe.ac.uk/genocide/yugoslav-hist1.htm> (11/1/2003).

Mihevc, Andrej. "Use of the Caves as Mass Graveyards in Slovenia." Karst Research Institute ZRC SAZU.

Ozic, Davorin. "The Bleiburg Tragedy!" May 6, 1968. <www.bleiburg.hrvati.net/>.

Serko, Alfred, and Ivan Michler. *The Postojna Grottoes and Other Marvels of the Karst*. Slovenia: Ljubljana, 1967.

Lewis Cave

Tudek, John. Personal communication, 2002.

Lijia Cave

Horn, Robert. "Bullion in Every Pot." *Time*, Feb. 2, 2002. <www.time.com/time/asia/arts/magazine/0,9754,107319,00.html> (10/31/2003).

Smart, Dean. "All that Glitters." *NSS News*, Oct. 2000.

Sukpanich, Tunya. "Treasure Hunt." *Bangkok Post*, May 13, 2001. <www.bangkokpost.net/>.

"Thailand Starts WWII Treasure Hunt." *CNN*, Apr. 16, 2001. <www.edition.cnn.com/2001/WORLD/asiapcf/southeast/04/16/thailand.treasure/> (10/31/2003).

"Thai Senator Lifts Lid on Treasure Trove." *CNN*, Apr. 16, 2001. <www.cnn.com/2001/WORLD/asiapcf/southeast/04/16/thai.treasure/> (10/31/2003).

Lobelia Saltpeter Cave

Balister, Rosemary. "A Gruesome Story from the Hills." *Illuminations*, Jan. 2002.

Cullinan, Mike. "What Ever Happened to Pete?" *Speleo Digest*. Alabama: National Speleological Society, 1976.

Hemple, Chuck. Personal communication, 2002.

Nagy, Bobbi. Personal communication, 2002.

Oldham, Tony. "The Enigma of Peter Hauer." *The British Caver*, Aug. 1976.

Sjaffer, C. R. "Report of Investigation No. 68611." West Virginia State Police.

Speece, Jack. "Pete: Peter Marshall Hauer: A Memorial." *Speleo Digest*. Alabama: National Speleological Society, 1976.

Loyang Cave

"Catanduanes." Provincial Profile of Catanduanes Website. <www.geocities.com/lppsec/pp/catanduanes.htm> (11/1/2003).

Macocha Abyss

Absolon, Karel B. *The Conquest of the Caves and Underground Rivers of Czechoslovakia's Macocha Abyss: A Historical and Technical Study of Their Exploration.* Maryland: Kabel Publishers, 1987.

"The Macocha Abyss." SMK Website. <www.smk.cz/uk/jeskyne/jmacocha.htm> (10/31/2003).

Oldham, Tony. "Punkva River Cave." Show Caves Website. <www.showcaves.com/english/cz/showcaves/Punkevni.html> (10/31/2003).

Makke'dah Cave

Holy Bible. New York: Thomas Nelson & Sons, 1952.

Mark Twain Cave

Weaver, H. Dwight. *Adventures at Mark Twain Cave.* Missouri: Discovery Enterprises, 1972.

Massacre Cave

"Behold the Hebrides: A Hebridean Tragedy: A Tale of an Eigg Cave." Electronic Scotland Website. <www.electricscotland.com/books/hebrides27.htm> (10/31/2003).

"Isle of Eigg History." Isle of Eigg Website. <www.isleofeigg.org/nature/geology.htm> (10/31/2003).

Love, John A. *Rum: A Land Without Figures.* Scotland: Birlinn Ltd., 2001.

Martin, Angus. "By Hill and Shore." The Kintyre Mag Website. <www.kintyremag.co.uk/1999/28/page8.html> (10/31/2003).

Oldham, Tony. *The Caves of Scotland.* Scotland, 1998.

Massacre Cave

"Canyon de Chelly National Monument." Desert USA Website. <www.desertusa.com/ind1/du_cdcdesc.html> (10/31/2003).

"Destinations: Canyon de Chelly National Park." Gorp Website. <www.gorp.com/>.

Reeves, T. K. "The Reprisals." <www.geocities.com/Yosemite/Trails/1942/reprisas.html> (10/31/2003).

Supplee, Charles. *Canyon de Chelly: The Story Behind the Scenery*. Nevada: KC Publications, 1990.

Massacre Island Cave

Leacock, Stephen. *The Mariner of St. Malo: A Chronicle of the Voyages of Jacques Cartier*. The Cumorah Project. E-Text. <www.cumorah.com/etexts/cca0210.txt> (10/31/2003).

"Massacre Island." Parc du Bic Website.<www.parcdubic.com/TexAg/P03BFh.htm> (10/31/2003).

Melidoni Cave

Koutsoupakis, Spyros. "A Brief History of Crete." <www.hep.physics.uch.gr/HistCrete.htm> (11/2/2003).

Oldham, Tony. "Melidoni Cave." *The British Caver*, July 1972.

Murphys Cave

"Army Hunts Boys in Cave." May 1967.

Dauner, John. "Persist in Efforts to Find Boys." *The Kansas City Star*, May 12, 1967.

Denkler, Susan. "Plaque Honors Those Lost in 1967 Tragedy." *Hannibal Courier-Post*, May 9, 1992.

"Eight-Day Million Dollar Search for Missing Boys is Abandoned." *Rolla Daily News*, May 17, 1967.

"Hope Dims for 3 Boys in Cave." May 13, 1967.

Kohnfelder, Earl. "Don't Give Up, Mothers Here Tell Cave Searchers for Boys." May 13, 1967.

"Mayor Feels Missing Boys are Not in Cave." May 18, 1967.

Miner, Michael. "Hannibal Boys Live in World of Twain."

Orthwein, Walter E. "Blast Opens Hannibal Cave in Search for 3 Lost Boys." *St. Louis Post-Dispatch*, May 27, 1967.

Swayzee II, Cleon. "Boys Sought at Road Project May Have Been Buried by Dirt." *St. Louis Post-Dispatch*, May 13, 1967.

Nickajack Cave

Cash, Johnny. *Cash: The Autobiography*. New York: Harper Collins, 1997.

Halliday, William R. *The Depths of the Earth*. New York: Harper & Row, 1966.

Ling, Roger. "Miracle at Nickajack." Station R Website. <www.cdc.net/~rling/rescues/nickajk.htm> (11/2/2003).

"Nickajack Lake Information." Tenneesee Lake Info Website. <www.tennesseelakeinfo.com/nickajacklake/> (11/2/2003).

Smith, Marion O. "Civil War Tour for Cavers Sewanee to Chattanooga." Lousiville, Tennessee, Byron's Graphic

Arts, 1998.
Ntavelis Cave
  Pantoulas, George N. "Ntavelis Cave Story." <www.v-jenterpris
    es.com/ntavelis.html> (11/2/2003).
Ofnet Cave
  Thorpe, Nick. "Origins of War: Mesolithic Conflict in Europe."
    British Archaeology, Apr. 2000. <www.britarch.ac.uk/ba/
    ba52/ba52feat.html> (11/2/2003).
Ouvea Cave
  Alailma, Kiali. "La Grotte D'Ouvea: The 1988 Massacre
    in the Cave of Gossannah, on the Island of Ouvea."
    <membres.lycos.fr/kanaky/news/martyrs.html> (11/2/2003).
  "Kanaky." Pacific Actions Website. <www.planet.org.nz/
    pacific_action/national/g_l/kanaky.html> (11/2/2003).
  "New Caledonia." Lonely Planet Website.<www.lonelyplanet.
    com/destinations/pacific/new_caledonia/history.htm>
    (11/2/2003).
Queho Cave
  Evans, K. J. "Part 1: The Early Years: Queho: Scoundrel or
    Scapegoat?" *Las Vegas Review-Journal*. <www.1st100.com/
    part1/queho.html> (11/2/2003).
  Hall-Patton, Mark. "Queho." June 21, 2003. <www.adcom.uci.
    edu/~sjweaver/queho.html> (11/2/2003).
Rattlesnake Cave
  Galonska, Juliet. "Rattlesnake Cave." Fort Smith National
    Historic Site Website. <www.nps.gov/fosm/history/radio/
    02.htm> (11/2/2003).
  Joenks, Laurinda. "Historian Recounts Wild West in Arkansas,
    Oklahoma." *The Morning News*, Sep. 15, 1999.
Rock House Cave
  Hammond, Cleon E. *John Hart: The Biography of a Signer of
    the Declaration of Independence*. Vermont: The Pioneer
    Press, 1977.
Sandanheki Cavern
  Humphries, Richard. "The Ghosts of Sandanheki." *Mainichi
    Daily News*, Japan Focus, May 20, 1998. <www2.gol.com/
    users/rick/article1/jaa1.html> (11/2/2003).
Sawney Beane Cave
  Rayner, J. L., and G. T. Crook. *The Complete Newgate
    Calendar*. London: Navarre Society, 1820.
  Oldham, Tony. *The Caves of Scotland*. Scotland, 1998.

Skeleton Cave

"Apache Campaigns: The Battle of Skull Cave." *Huachuca Illustrated.* Vol. 11. 1999.

"Battle with the Apache." History Through the Eyes of Those Who Lived it. EyeWitness to History Website. <www.eyewi tnesstohistory.com/apache.htm> (11/2/2003).

Machula, Paul R. "Hoo-Moo-Thy-Ah." <www.geocities.com/ ~zybt/boy.htm> (11/2/2003).

Nevin, David. *The Old West: The Soldiers.* New York: Time Life Books, 1974.

Skull Cave

Rea, Tom. "Mackinac Island." *National Speleological Society Official 1987 Guidebook, Sault Sainte Marie, Michigan,* 1987.

Wood, Edwin O. *Historic Mackinac: The Historical, Picturesque and Legendary Features of the Mackinac Country, Volume I.* New York: The Macmillan Company, 1918.

Suicide Cave

DeJean, Ed. "Suicide Cave." *Caving in the Heartland,* A Guidebook for the 1992 Convention of the National Speleological Society.